Hanover to Windsor

A volume in the British Monarchy series, which
also includes:

THE SAXON AND NORMAN KINGS
Christopher Brooke

THE TUDORS
Christopher Morris

THE STUARTS
J. P. Kenyon

THE FIRST FOUR GEORGES
J. H. Plumb

Royal Dukes

George IV

The Prince Consort

Queen Victoria

Votes for Women

The Greville Memoirs
(editor, with Lytton Strachey)

ROGER FULFORD

Hanover to Windsor

FONTANA/COLLINS

First published by B. T. Batsford Ltd 1960
First issued in Fontana Paperbacks 1966
Seventeenth impression January 1986

Copyright © Roger Fulford 1960

Made and printed in Great Britain by
William Collins Sons & Co. Ltd, Glasgow

PREFACE

This is the fourth volume in a series planned by Messrs. Batsford to cover the dynasties of British sovereigns. The Plantagenets, the Tudors, the Stuarts and the Hanoverian Georges have all been admirably treated, and the purpose of the present book (though it cannot strictly be called a dynastic history) is to bring the sequence down to modern times. The reason why this cannot be a dynastic history is that although the four sovereigns treated in this book are all nearly related they provide their historian with three separate dynasties. King William IV was the last sovereign of the House of Hanover, although Queen Victoria was a member of that House from the time of her accession until her marriage. With marriage the title of the Queen's house changed from Hanover to Saxe-Coburg-Gotha—to which dynasty Queen Victoria, King Edward VII and King George V all belonged. When the feeling against all things German was at its strongest in the dark days of the First World War, King George, yielding to clamour, changed the name of his dynasty from Saxe-Coburg-Gotha to Windsor. These various dynastic changes, though they were of no great consequence to the individuals concerned, have necessitated a departure from the simple standards governing the titles of the previous books in the series. The appearance of King William IV in this book also needs explanation. Although, by nature, King William IV belonged to the book dealing with the Georges, he helped to see through the parliamentary revolution of the Reform Bill and the effective transference of political power from the Crown to Parliament: this seemed to justify his inclusion with our later, more democratic rulers.

Contrasting the earlier books with this last one, the reader will notice how much has been written about these later sovereigns in comparison with members of the earlier dynasties. Consequently I have been more concerned to trace the position of the Crown and the standing of the monarchy through the lives of these four rulers than to repeat the gist of the excellent biographical studies of them which are available to every reader. Human curiosity being what it is, we like to know that George V telephoned to his sister every morning, that King Edward VII enjoyed mustard, that Queen Victoria was an ardent anti-vivisectionist and that King William forbade any water-drinking at his dining table. All those trifles (with many others) will be found in this book, but I have attempted to justify our enjoyment of such things by considering the impact on the institution of monarchy of the personality thus revealed. Indeed, does it not lend dignity to a personality, which may not necessarily have been very great or very fine, to draw that personality against a historical background and to consider the effect it may have had on the course of events? In tracing the lives of these rulers I have attempted to show the transition of the eighteenth-century monarchy to what it has become in the world to-day.

This book is not based on unpublished material, for the simple reason that what has been printed is ample for my purpose. I have, however, attempted to correct an oft-told tale about Queen Victoria when the Prince Consort died. I acknowledge, with gratitude, the gracious permission of Her Majesty the Queen to consult the Royal Archives on this point, and I thank Mr. Robin Mackworth-Young, the Librarian at Windsor, for his help. The sources for any statement of importance will be found in the body of the book, but I should like to emphasise my constant reliance on four books and for permission to quote from them. They are *The Letters of Queen Victoria* (John Murray); *King Edward VII,* by Sir Sidney Lee (Macmillan); *King George V—A Personal Memoir,* by John Gore (John Murray); and *King George V,* by Harold Nicolson (Constable). The authoritative life of Queen Mary by Mr. Pope-Hennessy was published after this book was finished. I am grateful to Messrs. Duckworth for allowing me to make use of some particulars from my book on the Royal Dukes, and I am also grateful to Messrs. Collins for having allowed me to draw on the book on Queen Victoria which I wrote for their series of Brief Lives in 1951.

August 1959

CONTENTS

ACKNOWLEDGEMENTS

The painting of Queen Victoria and Family by Winterhalter on the cover, the portraits of Queen Victoria in Later Life, Queen Victoria from a vignette by Sir Edwin Landseer, and Princess Victoria aged 15 from a vignette by R. J. Lane, the drawing of Queen Victoria at Buckingham Palace in 1841, the pictures of Queen and Prince in 1854, Queen Victoria and her Family in 1887, The Queen, Princess Louise and John Brown at Osborne, the Prince and Princess of Wales and their Children, the portraits of the Prince of Wales in 1875 and King Edward VII, the Duke of York in 1893, and the picture of King George at Cowes in 1935, are reproduced by gracious permission of Her Majesty The Queen.

The Author and Publishers wish to thank the following for permission to reproduce the illustrations appearing in this book: H.R.H. Prince Frederick of Prussia, and the Royal Library, Windsor, for the picture of King George at Cowes; the Ashmolean Museum, Oxford, for the picture of the silver crown coin of Queen Victoria; Fox Photos Ltd., for the picture of King George entering Hyde Park; the National Galleries of Scotland, for the portrait of King William IV by Sir David Wilkie; the National Portrait Gallery, for the portrait of Queen Adelaide by Sir William Beechey; Messrs Cassell & Co., for the picture of A Family and Imperial Group, which appeared in *The Royal Family by Pen and Camera* by Sarah A. Poole, 1907.

ILLUSTRATIONS

CHAPTER I

WILLIAM IV

Without being guilty of exaggeration an historian of the British monarchy could point to King William IV as its saviour. This strange, explosive, unpolitical and not clever sailor steered his course with capacity rather than brilliance, sensibly rather than subtly, through storms which were as wild and dangerous as those his father, King George III, had had to face during the worst political upheavals of his reign. He made his contribution to British history and takes his important place therein, not by any positive qualities but by being himself—in fact by existing at that particular moment. If he had died before 1830, or if he had never lived, the crown would have passed in 1830 to the infant Victoria, who was then eleven, under a Regency—a turn of events which would have strained the cohesion of the Royal Family, bitterly divided in politics as it was, and might well have led to those dynastic confusions which afflicted the girl queens of the Iberian Peninsula at that time. From such possibilities William IV saved the nation.

In addition to his own shortcomings for the Crown, he succeeded to it when its reputation stood far from high. His eldest brother, King George IV, the most accomplished of the Hanoverians and perhaps of all our sovereigns, had had to endure an eclipse of popularity and a torrent of abuse and ridicule unknown in English history. As a result of this, the reputation and authority of the Crown were severely damaged. To an extent King George had outlived his unpopularity, and when he died early in the morning of Saturday, 26 June 1830, an observer noticed that in London there were no signs of feeling, no sorrow, no joy—"only a bustle in the streets".[1] In fact King George, as a personality, was almost forgotten by his subjects. During the closing years of his life and reign he

[1]Lord Broughton, *Recollections of a Long Life*, 1909.

had remained at Windsor, an ailing recluse, attempting nothing more strenuous than a drive, in a pony carriage, from the Castle to his picturesque Gothic cottage—the Royal Lodge —or, if the weather was bright, driving as far as Virginia Water for an excursion on the water in his gaily painted barge, the expedition being rounded off by cherry-brandy and a cold collation in his fishing-temple there. The Home Park at Windsor was closed to the public; and soldiers ensured that the King's drives were completely secluded. He last went to Brighton, which had prospered famously under his patronage, in 1827 and left it for ever on 7 March that year. He came to London at rare intervals, and was last seen there in 1829, when he held a levée and gave a children's ball, which was attended by the future Queen Victoria. The contrast between this withdrawn and dispirited man and our later sovereigns with their gorgeous uniforms and gaily dressed consorts, waving and smiling to crowds, is absolute. Affability as one of the cardinal requisites for the sovereign of the British people came in with King William IV.

Succeeding, as he did, an unpopular and forgotten monarch, King William was given the chance to revive and restore monarchical feeling, yet that chance was complicated by hazards. For although King George had latterly neglected the outward form of Monarchy, had made no effort to keep the Kingship popular, he had fully maintained and perhaps enhanced the political authority of the Crown. Though never predictable, the King was nevertheless a force in politics. During his short reign, the cabinet of Lord Liverpool had tottered when it attempted to introduce Canning to the Government against the King's wishes: when Canning became Prime Minister he was greatly helped because the whole weight of the King's influence was thrown behind him: the King, with the help of certain foreign ambassadors, maintained a kind of independent foreign office at the Royal Lodge,[2] and, at the end of his life, his reluctance to agree to the emancipation of Roman Catholics very nearly brought Wellington's cabinet to the ground.

During his reign cabinet ministers had to brave the incon-

[2]This was known to the official world as "The Cottage Coterie".

venience of driving in their carriages the 20 miles from Whitehall to Windsor, for they knew that they must secure for their
measures the sanction and approval of the clever and capricious
master with whom they had to discuss affairs of state—not
infrequently while he was lying in bed. How would the dignity
and political authority of the Crown be maintained and how
would the country fare under the new King, who was almost
unknown to the public, had had no training for the throne
but was hopefully reported by those who knew him to be
"good-natured"?

When King William succeeded he was just short of sixty-
five, and there was at once a great hunting up of all the details
of his early life: authors snuffed around and produced little,
timely biographies: journalists, denied the resources of the
gossip-columnist and the carefully docketed archives of a
modern newspaper office, compiled paragraphs of anecdotes or
hinted at faded scandals. Surprisingly little was known, not a
great deal was invented but the new king emerged as primarily
a sailor, devoted to his sea-faring companions and the traditions
of the Royal Navy.

The Navy is seldom the best training for a sovereign, a point
often emphasised by King George V, who felt that the forth-
rightness instilled into all sailors is generally the worst weapon
for dealing with the subtleties of politics or the intransigence of
politicians. But King William's place in the family had
virtually dictated his future: he was born to be a sailor.
He was the third son of that family of fifteen princes and princesses founded by King George III and Queen Charlotte. He
first opened his eyes on 21 August 1765. King George III,
always strongly conservative in dynastic affairs, gave him the
same Christian names, William Henry, as had belonged to
his own father's third son. The careers of King William's
elder brothers were established from the cradle: the eldest to be
trained for his eventual succession to the throne, and the second
to be trained for command of the Army. The third, if physically
fit, must show that the King's affection for the Navy was as real
as his love for the Army. Thus it ever was. But if conservative in
dynastic matters, King George showed wisdom and breadth

of mind in deciding how his lively and attractive boy should be treated in his profession. In former times—Queen Anne's rather foolish husband is a case in point—princes had, as grown men, assumed the highest naval rank with no more than a nodding acquaintance with a man-o'-war. They achieved the brilliance of Admirals of the Red, Admirals of the Blue or Admirals of the White without having had to plant their sturdy legs on a quarter-deck. Not so Prince William. From boyhood he was to be a sailor prince, his youth bounded by a sea-faring life; the King, his father, with wisdom, felt that the country might well tire of having to find money for a string of royal dukes—resplendent in stars and ribands but idling through life. So when the prince was still only thirteen he became a midshipman on board the *Prince George,* which was lying in Portsmouth Harbour: he at once endeared himself to his shipmates by announcing to them that although he was entered on the ship's books as Prince William Henry he wished to be known always as William Guelph.[3] "I am nothing more than a sailor like yourselves," he added.

The start of his career was not unadventurous. In 1780 he served, under Rodney, in the relief of Gibraltar, bringing back to his delighted family some captured Spanish flags. In 1781 he sailed in the *Prince George* for America, and spent that winter in New York, which he was the first (and last) British prince to see while the Union Jack was still proudly flying over the thriving town. The district round New York was in the hands of the American independents, and Washington himself approved a plan (happily abortive) for capturing the sixteen-year-old prince; though with that respect for royal blood, which is a continuing characteristic of the American character, he insisted that the boy, if he was captured, should be treated with courtesy and without violence. Two years later he came home, and at once set out on a tour of central Europe—then unstained by revolution and still a happy land of Kings, electors, margraves and prince bishops enriching and beautifying their

[3]This is the historic patronymic of the Hanoverian Royal House. In the Nineteenth Century it was more correct for the Royal Family to use the name of Wettin—the patronymic of the Prince Consort.

domains and looking to the glories of Vienna as their capital
and its Emperor as their exemplar. The young prince was
politely received by his relative the great Frederick of Prussia
and also by the Emperor. As a lad in his teens he had seen
the last of the old world in all its European glory, and the
dawn of the new world across the Atlantic. When he was twenty-
one he was given the command of a frigate and served in the
West Indies, where he formed a close friendship with Nelson,
then a comparatively unknown captain. When Nelson made his
ill-starred marriage in Nevis the Prince gave away the bride
and said to the seemingly languid bridegroom: "I never saw a
lover so easy: it is not what is vulgarly called love."

In 1789 news reached him of his father's madness, and in
April of that year he was recalled to England. Although he
was devoted to his father and to his difficult, quick-tempered
mother he ranged himself with his two elder brothers in opposition to his parents. His elder brothers (the Prince of Wales
and Duke of York) felt that the moment the King's madness
declared itself the Regency should have devolved on the Prince
of Wales without discussion or hesitation. In fact the King re-
covered before the Regent was declared, and, on recovery,
he was wounded when he heard of the eagerness for power
displayed by his young sons. This split in the Royal Family
seems to be the reason why Prince William was punished by
being withdrawn from service at sea. With one short interval
of a few months in the 1820's, when he was Lord High
Admiral, he led the life, from the age of twenty-four till he
came to the throne at the age of sixty-five, which his father
had always wished him to escape; he was a royal duke with
expensive tastes but without any work. In 1789 his father
created him Duke of Clarence—a royal title which had been in
abeyance since Plantagenet times and whose last unhappy holder
had gained immortality through having supposedly met his end
in a butt of wine. He was given the subsidiary title of Duke
of Saint Andrews in Scotland and Earl of Munster in Ireland.
As his father signed the patent carrying these titles and a seat
in the House of Lords he sadly observed: "I well know that
it is another vote added to the Opposition." This was not

entirely just because, although the Duke of Clarence certainly sided with his elder brothers in dynastic disputes, he was not irretrievably a Whig. He stated in the House of Lords only three years later, when war with France was imminent; "I have already in private made an offer of my professional services to my country, and I am glad of an opportunity of expressing the same sentiments in public." But the offer was not accepted: the patriot prince was left to languish in the drawing-room. The reason for this is not absolutely clear, but the most likely explanation is that the Prince had reached a point in age and in his profession when he could not have gone to sea with a rank lower than that of admiral. While a royal general can avoid mistakes with a large staff of advisers, arrangements for controlling and advising a royal admiral at sea are more difficult and, taken in conjunction with the line which the Duke had followed over the Regency, explain why he was excluded from active service.

Although he may have been somewhat Whiggish in his political sympathies, the Duke was an intensely patriotic Englishman. George IV once said that he and his brother William were the only two of the royal princes who were completely English: the others, as King George pointed out, were all educated in Germany.[4] His devotion to Nelson was characteristic and constant: the two men were regular correspondents, the Duke was observed in tears at Nelson's funeral and he kept part of the foremast of the *Victory,* against which Nelson received his fatal wound, in his dining-room. He was in short an agreeable companion, a reliable friend and a thoroughly respectable prince.

But unluckily, as was the case with all his brothers, his amorous nature somewhat darkened the favourable picture, attracted a great deal of scurrility (not all of it forgotten when he came to the throne) and made him at times ridiculous. But before passing airy judgements on these private matters, the reader would do well to consider how Prince William and all his vigorous brothers were placed. They were cut off from Europe and its eligible princesses by the war with Napoleon,

[4]Creevey, vol. 1, p. 47.

and any natural desires which they may have had to marry
into the British aristocracy were curbed by a barbarous Act of
Parliament forced through the House of Commons by their
father in a moment of vexation. By that Act, the princes might
marry no one without the consent of their father, although
when they were twenty-five and wished to persist in a marriage to which the King objected they could appeal to Parliament. In the state of feeling on these topics, which prevailed
at that time, the King was most unlikely to agree to any marriage except to a royal princess. There was only a single individual—a rather stolid girl in her teens, who was the
Prince's first cousin—whom he could have married other
than a foreigner. To most minds, except those suited for the
austerities of a monastery, a liaison would seem not only
natural and inevitable but excusable.

Such a connexion the Prince quickly formed. He took under
his protection the beautiful and sparkling actress, Mrs. Jordan,
of whom Hazlitt wrote that: "She was the child of nature
whose voice was a cordial to the heart ... whose singing was
like the twang of Cupid's bow."[5] And in addition to all her
charms and graces Mrs. Jordan was strongly maternal and pre-
sented her husband with ten beautiful children—politely known
as the FitzClarences or to the censorious as "*les Bâtards*".

The Duke was Ranger of Bushy Park, and in that attractive, well-timbered setting he made his home. For twenty years
he lived here a retired life, with his family, only interrupted by
Mrs. Jordan's frequent returns to the stage—of which he disapproved. He was, however, powerless to forbid her continued
acting because the money she earned was extremely helpful
in maintaining their joint establishment—a state of affairs which
went some way to justify the question: "Does he keep her
or she keep him?"

The Duke would, no doubt, have continued this happy
domestic existence with Mrs. Jordan, for the span of time pre-
scribed by the Church's marriage service. Two reasons prevented him from this. The first and most compelling one was
the lack of money; if he made a marriage, which was approv-

[5]Hazlitt, *Dramatic Essays*, 1851.

ed, his allowance from Parliament would have been inevitably increased. The other reason was the realisation that the electorate of Hanover must almost certainly fall to him and his legitimate, male descendants.[6] Thoughts of the future occupied the minds of the Royal Family when the King's mind finally broke down in 1811, and it was in that year, with some precipitation, that the Duke broke with Mrs. Jordan. She wrote to a friend excusing the Duke's conduct with the words, "Money, Money". He is believed to have made her the generous allowance of £2,000 a year, and if that was rather irregularly paid, some of the blame for such irregularity might not unfairly be laid at the door of the Duke's rather tiresome creditors.

From henceforward his proposals of marriage were to ring through Europe with something of the same monotony as did the cannon of Napoleon. They caused much gossip and amusement at the time, and such documentary evidence as has survived suggests that both the laughter and the chatter were amply justified. After abortive offers to wealthy English ladies, to Russian and German princesses the Duke was still single in 1815. The final defeat of Napoleon had opened the Continent to English princes eager to engage in what an amusing writer called "Hymen's war terrific". In November of that year the Duke wrote to his eldest brother to say that he was ready and happy to set out for the Continent the moment you please, "as I have not any doubt that the eldest daughter of Landgrave Frederick of Hesse is a lady in every respect fit to be my wife". But the Landgrave, a grandson of King George II, was less confident: in royal French he wrote to the Regent "*que tant la jeunesse de ma fille que la constitution délicate, comme la nombreuse famille du Duc de Clarence avancé dans un âge mûr, me fait espérer qu'il ne vienne pas de proposition de noce en forme pour cet effet.*"[7] Two years later the poor Duke was still without his bride. The matter had now taken a desperate turn,

[6]The Princess Charlotte, being a woman, could not succeed in Hanover nor pass the succession to her children. Unless the Prince Regent or the Duke of York, whose wife was childless, remarried, the Hanoverian succession must have come to the Duke of Clarence and his male heirs.

[7]*Letters of George IV*, edited by Professor Aspinall, vol. ii, pp. 247-8.

for the death of Princess Charlotte, without surviving children, meant that unless his elder brothers re-married (which was most unlikely) he would be inevitably King of both England and Hanover.[8]

Unfortunately he had fallen desperately in love with an English heiress—Miss Wykeham—who was considered by her contemporaries as "half-crazy". Though respectable she was regarded as totally unsuitable to be the Duke's wife by both the Regent and the Government, who forbade the marriage.[9] It was at this juncture, with the Duke deeply enamoured of an unsuitable lady, that the heiress to the throne, Princess Charlotte, died and it became imperative that he should forthwith make an appropriate marriage and provide the nation with an heir. The affair was desperate, and piteously he wrote to his mother —the old but still formidable Queen Charlotte: "I have ten children totally dependent on myself: I owe £40,000 for which of course I pay interest, and I have a floating debt of £16,000."[10] He added—and for this posterity must applaud him—that he would not even consider marriage unless he might see his daughters by Mrs. Jordan as and when he wished. On 21 March 1818 he wrote to his eldest illegitimate son: "I have delayed till the last moment writing in hopes of being able to inform you who is to be the Duchess of Clarence. I can now with *truth* tho' not with *satisfaction* my heart being with Miss Wyckham. It is to be the Princess of Saxe-Meiningen, whose *beauty* and *character* are *universally* acknowledged. She is doomed *poor, dear, innocent young* creature to be my wife. I *cannot, I will not*, I *must not* ill use her. . . . What time may produce in my heart I can not tell, but at present I *think* and exist only for Miss Wyckham. But enough of your father's misery."[11]

[8]Hanover had moved up from an electorate to a kingdom after the Napoleonic Wars.

[9]To his credit King William created Miss Wykeham a peeress in her own right as the Baroness Wenman when he came to the throne. She lived at Thame Park, near Oxford, and died unmarried in 1870.

[10]*Letters of George IV*, edited by Professor Aspinall, vol. II, p. 227.

[11]*Mrs. Jordan and Her Family*, edited by A. Aspinall, 1951, to which the reader's attention is directed for an elaboration of the Duke's private life. The Duke's spelling of Wykeham is unorthodox.

Few marriages, either royal or common, can have started less propitiously; the Duke's nuptials opened to the accompaniment of tears and sighing more appropriate for the graveyard. Princess Adelaide was the daughter of the reigning duke of the "pocket-duchy" of Saxe-Meiningen, just north of Coburg, whose ruler was an off-shoot of the Saxon royal house. She accepted her difficult husband with his train of debts and bastards, made him an admirable wife and gave the British people an exemplary Queen Consort. Her only drawback was that she failed to provide her husband with living issue—her two daughters dying in babyhood.

For the next ten years of his life the Duke lived in semi-retirement at Bushy, with his amiable consort, who throughout life was unfailingly kind to the FitzClarence children. The great events of the 1820's—the trial of Queen Caroline, the flamboyant foreign policy of Canning or the agitation for the Emancipation of Roman Catholics—passed him by.

In 1827 his next brother, the Duke of York, died and he became heir presumptive. The King and the Government marked the occasion by creating him Lord High Admiral —an office comparable with Commander-in-chief of the Army which demanded both leadership of the forces and administration in Whitehall. The office itself was something of an anachronism, since it had been last filled by the husband of Queen Anne, more than a century previously. The Duke was successful in the active work of his office, visiting the dockyards with assiduous informality and on occasion running up the Lord High Admiral's flag and leading out a squadron of ships to sea. But his quick, Hanoverian temper could not tolerate the Board of the Admiralty (mostly civilians) with whom he had to work, and on one occasion the Duke and a squadron of ships were at sea without anyone knowing the whereabouts of the ships. The Government told the King that unless the Duke resigned they could not continue in office. So after a short but glorious official life of fifteen months he resigned, and retired to bed for a week to recover from the excitement.

Compassionate persons might think it wrong to dwell over-

much on the oddities of the Duke—for in addition to being
odd he was good-hearted, unselfish and given neither to intrigue nor malice—yet his conduct over his abortive marriages
and as Lord High Admiral caused much comment; moreover,
they form an essential preamble to an understanding of both
his shortcomings and achievements as King. Those within the
private circle of the Court were apprehensive of his capacity
for the Crown. Even his eldest brother shared these feelings,
and he wrote to the Prime Minister at the time of the rum-
pus over the Lord High Admiral. "I love my brother
William, I have always done so to my heart's core: and I will
leave him the example of what the duty of a King of this
country really is." And he added that he must either obey the
laws of Parliament or else resign. Though never badly intentioned, the Duke, when thwarted, was capable of wildness
and silliness. And this explains why one, who surveyed the
whole official and aristocratic world with an observant though
possibly jaundiced eye, could write of the Duke: "At present
he is only a mountebank, but he bids fair to be a maniac."[12]

Though exaggerated and severe such language was not altogether out of place in describing the opening days of his
reign, when he stepped to the front as King William IV of
Great Britain and I of Hanover. When he drove up to London
from Bushy on the morning after King George IV's death, he
was wearing a white hat from the crown of which was flying
a streamer of black crêpe—known in the language of the day
as "a weeper". But far from weeping the new King was smiling
and bowing to such of his subjects as chanced to look in
his direction. At the first meeting of the Privy Council—when
the Privy Councillors gathered to swear allegiance to their
new king, he behaved with dignity, spoke with affection of
his brother, but destroyed the good impression by saying in
an audible aside to the clerk, as he signed his name: "This is
a damn'd bad pen you have given me." At the late King's
funeral he was chief mourner and as, enveloped in a sweeping
black cloak, he followed the massive coffin up the length of
St. George's Chapel at Windsor he alarmed the company by

[12]Greville, vol. II, p. 18.

recognising various friends and giving them a hearty hand-shake. A few days later he decided to take a stroll down St. James's Street, unattended by any of his courtiers: he was quickly recognised, hustled and cheered, and it is whispered that a courageous lady of the streets was able to salute her new sovereign with a kiss on the cheek. When he was rescued he said: "Oh, never mind all this: when I have walked about a few times they will get used to it." (Later members of the English Royal Family would hardly agree with this sanguine forecast of the ease with which publicity could be avoided.) When the Coronation came up for discussion the new king scandalised Conservative opinion by declaring it "a useless and ill-timed expense". He wished to do away with the cere-mony altogether, and only agreed to a Coronation if it could be managed at a fraction of the cost of King George IV's. His was the first Coronation at which the great banquet in Westminster Hall was abandoned—with lordly dishes carried in, preceded by the great Officers of State on horseback and enlivened by the ceremony of the challenge. And for this reason and its general air of frugality King William's Coro-nation was dubbed by the wits "the half-crownation"—but it has formed the precedent for subsequent ceremonies. When the Tory peers, shocked by these prunings of antique flum-mery, threatened to absent themselves from the ceremony the King merely observed that he thought that this would be con-venient, since there would be "more room and less heat". However, all observers agree that few of our sovereigns have had a warmer or more whole-hearted greeting from the crowd than the King and Queen when they drove down to the Abbey for their truncated Coronation.

He was, it will be seen, an unconventional sovereign, re-luctant to do as he was told and indifferent to the traditions of his office: he believed that he could best serve the nation by being natural and by not handing over his personality bound and gagged to the etiquette of the Court. He could not, for example, understand that when he was driving in London he must not ask one of the Lords-in-waiting to sit beside him: he was expected to sit alone, his attendants opposite with their backs to the horses. To those outside the circles of Courts such things are trifling, but his disregard of them was of a piece with his sudden explosions, his turkey-cock ejaculations and eagerness to harangue people on the least provocation: all these characteristics invited that question, highly damaging to any official personage, "What on earth will he do next?" Such conduct unquestionably diminished the dignity of the Crown, and the misfortune was that he had no natural dignity to replace that which was lost.

Shorter than the rest of his family, with the wide mouth and features of his mother, Queen Charlotte, a very red face and a pear-shaped head he looked what he was—a fidgety retired naval officer, perhaps only really at ease on the quarterdeck; he seemed, as the head of a state, to be, as his niece Queen Victoria observed, "very odd and singular".[13]

This very singularity helped, for there is no surer way to popularity in England than to be a character—to be the kind of person of whom anecdotes are told. Especially is this true of a crowned character. In most cases the conversations of ordinary mortals with royal persons are of imponderable insipidities. Subjects come away from a chat with their sovereign with nothing more enduring to repeat to their friends than embroidered examples of their own brilliance or their own gaucheries. In King William's time this was different. He generally gave those he honoured with his conversation a great deal to remember and some spicy anecdotes for their friends. At Brighton he was fond of looking up his old naval cronies, and inviting them to dinner at the Pavilion, which, in his brother's time, had been renowned for the brilliant formality of the entertainments. "Come along directly," he would say, "do not bother about clothes. The Queen does nothing but embroider flowers after dinner."[14] On another occasion he was asked which horses he would like to enter from the royal stables for a certain race, and he replied: "Send down the whole squadron." His views on art were likewise memorable, and he gave it as his opinion that "all pictures of sacred subjects are improper and

[13]*Girlhood of Queen Victoria,* edited by Lord Esher, vol. I, p. 194.
[14]Doran, *Queens of England of the House of Hanover,* vol. II, p. 434.

ought to be destroyed."[15] He was always incapable of reticence, loved talking volubly to people and perhaps imagined he was putting them at their ease. At the end of an evening party he turned to the assembled company and said: "Now ladies and gentlemen I wish you a good night. I will not detain you any longer from your amusements, and shall go to my own which is to go to bed. So come along my Queen."[16] When he was entertaining a private party at the Pavilion on the last day of 1832 he called for a country dance to celebrate the new year. To the amazement of his guests he seized an old Admiral of the White, Lord Amelius Beauclerk, for his partner. The sight of these two veterans going down the middle, hand in hand, was truly farcical. He had the full share of that quick temper of the English Royal Family and made no effort whatever to control it. One of his most remarkable outbursts was when he was looking over the pictures of the Royal Academy in 1834: the President of the Academy paused to show the King the portrait of the distinguished naval officer Admiral Napier. At that time Napier was under criticism for intervening in the Portuguese civil war by commanding the ships on the Liberal side. The trembling President was alarmed when the King, pausing in front of the painting, exploded: "Captain Napier may be damn'd, sir. And you may be damn'd, sir, and if the Queen was not here, sir, I would kick you downstairs."[17] Though frightening at the time this outburst made a refreshing change from the banalities of royal chat, and the popularity of King William was not greatly diminished by this and countless similar anecdotes which were told of him.

Although it would be tedious to detail the occasions on which the King made official visits in and around London, Brighton and Windsor, these were an innovation and played an important part in popularising the monarchy. He never went very far afield, and he attempted nothing in the way of a modern provincial tour undertaken by our twentieth-century sovereigns. He paid, for example, an official visit to Lewes from Brighton soon after his accession, and the visit was noteworthy because

[15]*Girlhood of Queen Victoria,* edited by Lord Esher, vol. II, p. 231.
[16]Greville (1938 edition), vol. II, p. 13.   [17]Doran, vol. II, p. 455.

he explained to the Mayor that his brother, who was popular in that part of Sussex, had been little seen during his reign because of a collapse in health. In 1831 he opened the new London Bridge, and was given a great ovation. Anyone looking through the newspapers of those times will find constant descriptions of their Majesties and suite driving out with a string of half a dozen carriages, escorted by the Life Guards or a Lancer regiment. He loved going down the Thames in the Royal Barge to Woolwich. Was he perhaps the first of our Hanoverian kings to attend the marriage of a subject? This was the wedding of the Duke of Wellington's nephew, Lord Cowley, at St. George's, Windsor, where the King signed the register. All this bustle and activity spread and strengthened loyal feeling to the sovereign.

In view of what lay ahead this was as well, because the country had no sooner settled down to the enjoyment of its new sovereign than a political storm, which had been long brewing, burst with alarming violence and with the prospect of long-continuing mischief over the heads of King and Parliament. For half a century the grievances of Whigs, liberals and radicals had been voiced in the House of Commons but had found no response in the Government of the day. First the twenty-year struggle with Napoleon and then the nervousness of revolutionary outbreaks after the war had fortified conservative resistance to all reform—to any concession to popular clamour. Though the years from 1780–1831 were among the glorious ones of English history, politically they were becalmed. The ship of state moved across the waters, heavily defended, bristling with repellent cannon and manned with a crew whose concern was neither to adventure nor to explore but to survive. All around them seethed new ideas, plans for reform and schemes for ending abuses: they swirled along Fleet Street: they penetrated the City of London: they were on all men's tables in the writings of Byron and the Lake poets and in the strident articles of the Reviews. And broadly speaking all these diverse plans were caught up in one idea; all those inspiring them were united in concentrating on a single objective—the reform of Parliament and the extension of the vote to a wider fran-

chise, to classes excluded from any share in the government
of their nation. All happiness, all prosperity were to flow
from this measure. "This Reform will touch everybody by and
by," George Eliot makes one of her characters say; "a thoroughly popular measure—a sort of A.B.C. that must come first
before the rest can follow."[18]

Within a few weeks of William IV's accession two events
occurred which combined to sweep away the cautious Conservatives from power and to admit the full force of the pent-up
reforming excitement of the Opposition. The first was the over-
throw of the Bourbons in France, the establishment of popular
government there and the revival of those stirring memories,
associated with the outbreak of the Revolution forty years
earlier, which gave their decided fillip to revolutionary thought
in this country. At that time the accession of a new sovereign
necessitated a general election in Great Britain: the news from
France arrived in the middle of the poll: the Conservatives
lost 50 seats, leaving the Duke of Wellington's Tory Government poised on the edge of a precarious majority.

The second event was fatal to Wellington's government, and
might well have proved fatal to King William. A new king,
in those days, paid a visit of respect to the City of London
on succeeding to the throne, and it was customary for him
to do this by dining with the Lord Mayor on 9 November at
Guildhall.[19] Two days before the visit was due, when all the
arrangements were made, when the bunting was in place and
each portly alderman had hired an ambling nag to bear him
in triumph before his king, the Lord Mayor suddenly wrote
to the Prime Minister, Wellington, saying that there were
some desperate characters at large and that if the Duke was
accompanying the King he should come "strongly and sufficiently guarded". The Government decided to abandon the whole
visit and, when news of this was known, crowds congregated
in the City, arms were purchased and shutters fixed by nervous citizens. Consols fell three points. The King, who certainly
had nothing to fear, was furious with Wellington for pre-

[18]Mr. Brooke in George Eliot's *Middlemarch*.
[19]This agreeable custom seems to have been dropped by King Edward VII.

venting him from going to the City, and when eight days
later the Government failed to defeat a hostile vote in the House
of Commons he sent for the Whigs—without regret. At the
end of November the new Government was formed with Grey
as Prime Minister, Brougham as Lord Chancellor and Lord
John Russell in the Ministry: it was clearly a Reform Government, the inclusion of Lord John showed that it meant business
and that it was going to pull down the blind on the half century
of reaction.

Although the King was not unreasonably nervous (for he
was certainly no enthusiast for any sweeping schemes of reform)
he threw his influence behind the new Government. In those
days a sovereign identified himself with his Government to an
extent which is not easily understood in the twentieth-century,
when we are accustomed to a ruler who, in the midst of the
political tussle, behaves with the air and impartiality of a
referee. Not only did King William appoint Whigs to the
chief places at Court but his entertaining was virtually confined
to the Government: Tories were excluded, except on the most
formal and official occasions, from any contact with their King.

Throughout 1831 the King gained great popularity by his
steady adherence to the Reforming Government. He gave the
Prime Minister a signal mark of his confidence by creating
him an extra member of the Order of the Garter, although
there was no vacancy. When there was only a majority of a
single vote in favour of the Reform Bill in the House of Commons, he exercised, without demur, his prerogative of dissolving Parliament although it had not been in existence for more
than nine months. The decision to dissolve had to be taken
hurriedly, and the courtiers complained that there would be
no time to get the coach ready and arrange for the sovereign's
escort of cavalry customary on these occasions. In the midst of
this palaver King William turned to Grey and said: "My
Lord, I'll go if I go in a hackney-carriage." And that amusing
and enthusiastic Whig, Creevey, wrote with gusto of what he
called "our Billy's courage and fidelity".[20]

But both his courage and his fidelity were to be put to a

[20]*Creevey's Life and Times*, edited by John Gore, p. 343.

sharper test as 1831, that triumphant year for the Reformers which had also seen the Coronation, drew to its close. The Bill had passed the new House of Commons with large majorities, but it was rejected by the House of Lords, and it became clear that a dispute between the two houses would be inevitable. Throughout all parts of the country there were disturbances, and the King had the disagreeable experience of being jeered and hooted when he drove back from the theatre—one of the mob throwing a stone through the carriage window which fell in the lap of the King's nephew—Prince George of Cumberland, afterwards the last King of Hanover. Though physically brave the King was by nature undecided and nervous. "He was a very timid man—very easily frightened," Lord Melbourne told Queen Victoria.[21] Increasing disorder as the year advanced and the fear that he was opening the door to extremism made the King hesitate in support of the Whig Government and unluckily destroyed the good relations established between them.

With 1832 the Government saw that they could not hope to secure the passage of the Bill into law unless they could persuade the King to use his constitutional powers—that is to say to create sufficient new peers to out-vote the opponents of the Bill in the Lords. Now for many reasons the King disliked this possibility and always referred to it as "the dreaded alternative". King William was, it will be seen, in a position of delicacy. If he agreed to create the necessary peers—some fifty or sixty—he would certainly antagonise the opponents of the Bill and also all those Conservative forces in the country which were the buttresses of the monarchy. Through the Queen, through the higher clergy, through his illegitimate children, through old seafaring friends and through reading Opposition newspapers he was perfectly aware of how he would be criticised and condemned, if he placed this ultimate sanction of the Crown behind the Whig Government, and his spirits quailed at the prospect. Was he perhaps like John Gilpin clutching nervously at his mount and quite uncertain when he would be thrown or when his journey would end? He spent the Christmas of 1831 at the Pavilion in Brighton

[21]*Girlhood of Queen Victoria*, edited by Lord Esher, vol. 1, p. 283.

—that splendid creation of his brother, with the mandarins leering at him from the walls and the dragons coiled above his head. In this cheerful setting, he received the Prime Minister and, with the greatest reluctance, agreed to create peers to force the Bill through—provided there was no permanent addition to the number of peers. This was to be avoided by only calling up the heirs of Whig peers, and by drawing on Scottish and Irish peers favourable to the Bill. Here it can be argued that the King made his mistake. He agreed to what he disliked and, as is the way of all human beings when they are unsure of themselves, he accompanied it with niggling qualifications. With political passions at the boil the country was not likely to distinguish between a general agreement and this limited one. The truth of this was shown in the early summer of 1832. The Government was defeated in the Lords, Grey went to the King and explained that the limited class would not provide enough new peers to overpower the Opposition. He then asked for an unlimited creation and said that he would have to resign if that was not forthcoming. With tears the King accepted Grey's resignation. Even a well-informed observer like Creevey wrote: "Our beloved Billy cuts a damnable figure." And to the mob outside the King became damnable indeed. He drove up from Windsor to London, strongly guarded by a posse of cavalry, but pelted by clods of dirt from a crowd yelling and hooting to the full extent of their brazen lungs. He found it impossible to form any alternative Government, and in the result he had to send for Grey and agree to all demands. He gave the Royal Assent to the Reform Bill on 7 June 1832. Greville said that as a result of this episode "the regal authority" had fallen into contempt. He added that the personal unpopularity of King George IV never degraded the Kingly office, because as King he was able to cancel the bad impression which he made in his individual capacity.

In order to judge this matter fairly—and it affected the course of monarchical power in England—the reader should forget all the benign consequences which are thought to have flowed from the Reform Bill and consider the feelings of thoughtful Conservative opponents of the Bill. They felt that the pro-

posals were revolutionary but that they were hampered in
resisting them after the King seemed to lend them his
authority. Had he not agreed—they asked themselves—to a
dissolution and to the creation of peers? By continuing their
opposition after such a clear expression of royal approval would
they not be justly accused of dragging down the King into the
thick of the fray? The point was well put immediately after
King William's death by a writer who was plainly a Conservative partisan. "Had William the Fourth, with less natural
intelligence, been endowed with something of that instinct of
self-defence and distrust, which the weakest animals have com-
monly the largest share of, the part he might have taken in
the crisis would probably have been a much wiser one, not for
himself and his crown merely but for the country and the constitution."[22] Not dissimilarly the Whigs felt that the King had
played them false, seeming to agree to a creation of peers at
the Pavilion in the winter and then going back on it at
Windsor in the summer. The unpleasant difficulties in which
King William found himself, help to explain why our later
sovereigns have been increasingly reluctant to take advantage
of these prerogatives of the Crown, except as an absolutely last
resort.[23]

In justice to the King this must be said. He felt that his
Government (in whom he had shown exceptional confidence)
had been heedless of his position, lost him popularity at a
critical time and exposed him to public vilification. The events

[22]*Annual Register*, 1837, p.236.
[23]Those who wish to follow this matter more closely should look at the
correspondence between the King and Grey which was edited by Henry
Lord Grey and published in two volumes in 1867. The King's letters in
this collection reveal him in a favourable light – though some of the credit
must belong to his private secretary – Sir Herbert Taylor. Apart from the
time when George III was going blind this was the first occasion that an
English sovereign had a secretary recognised by the Government as a
channel of communication for official business. Taylor was a sound and
disinterested man on whom the King implicitly relied. Melbourne told
Queen Victoria that Taylor could turn the King any way. "That was a
wrong thing," observed the young Queen. Wrong it may have been but
the whole correspondence reflects the effort which the King made to be
reasonable, the good sense of Taylor and the moderation of Grey.

of 1832 soured him and embittered him. His fears encouraged by the Queen,[24] and by his sisters who well remembered the stormy battles of their father's time, he pictured events as moving at a gallop to revolution and that it was for him to draw the rein and pull them in. "I feel the Crown tottering on my head," he once said. For this uncomfortable feeling he blamed his ministers: he was waiting for revenge.

Two years later the chance came. In the spring of 1834, Grey, who had occupied the first place with great distinction, resigned and was succeeded as Prime Minister by Melbourne, who like Grey was in the Lords. In the autumn the leader of the House of Commons succeeded to a peerage and Melbourne in the familiar setting of *chinoiserie* at Brighton, told the King that he proposed to appoint Lord John Russell as leader of the House of Commons. "I cannot bear John Russell,"[25] the King had told Melbourne; and in private he had said: "If you will answer for his death, I will answer for his damnation." At bay he turned on his tormentors and dismissed the Government. "This is the greatest piece of folly ever committed", wrote an able observer from the Whig side.[26] That this was the case is suggested by the fact that the dismissal of a Government has never been attempted since that day by any of the King's successors on the throne. Chaos ensued. Peel, the new Prime Minister, was enjoying an artistic excursion in Rome, and the Duke of Wellington acted as a caretaker Premier. The new Government appealed to the country in the spring of 1835, and lived a precarious existence till May, when it was defeated and the King, with the best grace he could muster, had to accept the Whigs back with Lord John as leader of the House of Commons.

The King had in fact been roundly snubbed. He had forced a general election and—to use a phrase of Melbourne's—the Crown had had its opponents "returned smack against it". The full extent of the King's apprehensions—and it was these

---

[24]Here it is fair to add that Grey maintained that the Queen had no influence over the King except by way of improving his manners.
[25]Spencer Walpole, *Life of Lord John Russell*, Longmans, 1889. [26]*Ibid*.

which made him bitterly hostile to the Whigs—are revealed
by his attitude to two issues in the closing years of his reign.
Although he was not conspicuously a religious man he had
the feelings of respect for the authority and influence of the
Church of England which marked his family and his generation. He felt that the Whigs were planning to subvert the
church, to trim its privileges and to seize some of its treasure.
He was not alone in this. Oxford rang the tocsin in 1833 with
Keble's celebrated assize sermon about the threat to the Churches
from the Whig government. With the King these feelings went
even deeper because, in addition to his loyalty to the Church,
he regarded it as the foundation of the Constitution and the
buttress of his family's right to the throne. In one of his celebrated, impromptu speeches—made to a gathering of Irish
bishops in May 1834—he elaborated these points with all his
explosive vigour. After saying that he had not known what
sickness was for some years, he emphasised that as he was
sixty-eight he could not expect to live much longer: he well
knew that according to law he could do no wrong but that
only made him the more sensible of "the responsibility under
which I stand to the Almighty Being. . . . The threats of those,
who are enemies of the Church, make it the more necessary
for those who feel their duty to the Church to speak out. The
words which you hear from me are, indeed, spoken by my
mouth but they flow from the heart."[27]

He felt indeed that the outlook of the Whigs on the Church
was of a piece with their indifference to the well-tried principles of the Constitution. It was this which gave rise to the
second outburst, which occurred in the following year—1835.
Three Commissioners were appointed by the Government to
enquire into the affairs of Canada which were at that time
disturbed. The three Commissioners attended the King at St.
James's Palace to be sworn in as Privy Councillors. Turning to
one of them the King spoke thus: "Stand up. Sir Charles Grey
—you are about to proceed upon one of the most important mis-
sions which ever left this country, and, from your judgement,
ability and experience I have no doubt that you will acquit

[27] *Annual Register*, 1834.

yourself to my entire satisfaction: I desire you, however, to bear in mind that the colony to which you are about to proceed has not, like other British Colonies, been peopled from the Mother Country—that it is not an original possession of the Crown, but that it was obtained by *the sword*. You will take care to assert those undoubted prerogatives which the Crown there possesses and which I am determined to enforce and maintain, and I charge you by the oath which you have just taken strenuously to assert the prerogative, of which persons who ought to have known better have dared even in my presence to deny the existence."[28]

Examples of his oratory still delight all observers of human nature. At a large dinner he said: "Ever since I came to the throne I have liked to assemble at my table all sorts of people. Therefore I now give you the health of the Bishop of London." At a military dinner he emphasised the comprehensive nature of the army by addressing Lord FitzRoy Somerset: "You, my Lord, are descended from the Plantagenets," and then turning to Sir James Kempt: "And you are descended from the very dregs of the people." Kempt was one of Wellington's Peninsula generals.

Although the King was still capable of astonishing indiscretions—he once said that he would sooner entertain the devil than have any of the ministers in his house—relations with his Government steadied down in the two years of life which remained to him.

And, in private life, after the excitements of the early months of his reign he also steadied down to an unordered and unvarying routine. He slept in the same room with Queen Adelaide—though in a separate bed. He was called at 7.45 and took an eternity over dressing and his ablutions. He sat down to breakfast at 9.30 and drank a single cup of coffee, eating two fingers of toast. After breakfast he read carefully *The Times* and the *Morning Post,* exclaiming with indignation if he came

[28]Greville (1938 edition), vol. III, p. 218. The King was referring to the Secretary of State for the Colonies (Lord Glenelg), a foolish man, but Melbourne had to tell the King afterwards that the Government could not carry on if they were to be subjected to these outbursts.

on something of which he disapproved. (When he came across a paragraph in one of those respectable journals that the Queen was expecting a child he was heard to roar out, "Damn'd stuff.") He then worked steadily with his private secretary till 2 p.m., when he had luncheon. The menu was unvaried—two cutlets and two glasses of sherry. He then went out for a drive. At dinner he ate sparingly: he drank no wine except sherry, of which he consumed a bottle.

He did not like his guests to drink water. When King Leopold of the Belgians was staying with him he suddenly called across the table: "What's that you are drinking, sir?" "Water, sir," replied the Belgian king. "God damn it, why don't you drink wine? I never allow anybody to drink water at my table."

Punctually at 11 p.m. he went to bed. To the Royal Family he was a kindly and affectionate head, devoted in particular to the children of his brothers, including his successor Princess Victoria. Thirty years later Queen Victoria publicly recalled: "Of his kindness to herself, and his wish that she should be duly prepared for the duties to which she was so early called, the Queen can only speak in terms of affectionate gratitude."[29] The future Queen's mother, the Duchess of Kent, he loathed. He treated her on one occasion to a terrible salvo of royal oratory, saying that she was incompetent and that she had grossly and continually insulted him. This took place at the King's birthday dinner at Windsor Castle. Rustling her silks and satins and taking the Princess Victoria, who was in tears, the Duchess fled from the castle. Among other comments the King, on this occasion, said that he hoped to God his life might be spared till the Princess came of age so that there would be no question of her mother being Regent. This wish was granted. He lived for a month after the Princess's eighteenth birthday, in 1837, dying slowly from a disorder of the circulation but with courage. With their bland falsifications, the doctors let it be known that the King was suffering from hayfever; Mr. Disraeli, in his novel Sybil, reminds us that the official world was not deceived. A political lady assured her

[29]Martin, Life of the Prince Consort, vol. II, p. 177.

friend: "The poor dear King will never show again." As the anniversary of the Battle of Waterloo came round he said to his doctors: "I know that I am going, but I should like to see another anniversary of Waterloo. Try if you cannot tinker me up to last over that date." Two days later he died, murmuring, "The Church, the Church." So died King William IV, the Sailor King—not perhaps a great ruler but good-hearted, human and a patriot. He was the link joining our modern sovereigns with the more politically powerful Georges. He had to face great difficulties—some inherent in his own character but most of them deriving from the politics of his reign. The powers of the Crown were diminished when he was on the throne as a result of these struggles, but he will be remembered by posterity as one who made his contribution to the modern monarchy and in his bluff, natural way enhanced its popularity.

CHAPTER II

QUEEN VICTORIA

Queen Victoria—to a greater extent than most British sovereigns —was fashioned by the monarchy. The impact of influence, power and authority on the mind of an unformed girl not only moulded her character but, throughout her long reign of sixty-three years, modified it. For one of the most fascinating sides of the Queen's character lies in its curious contradiction. She was stubborn but she was not inflexible. To her mother, her children and grand-children, to her courtiers and ministers she showed a side of her nature which was steely, but to circumstances and changes in her surroundings she was far less hard—indeed she changed as they changed. In personal relations she was adamant, but to her environment she was adaptable. So much is this the case that there are five distinct Victorias— the sheltered, rather down-trodden Princess, the gay young Queen, the devoted wife, the abject widow and finally the symbol of British glory at its zenith. Although the changes may have been gradual and imperceptible, each character is perfectly distinct from its predecessor, and she herself seems to have been almost conscious of these changes and of the drama of life, which fashioned her before the world. In one of the first letters which she wrote after the death of the Prince Consort she opens with a description of herself as "the poor fatherless baby of eight months" being "now the utterly broken-hearted and crushed widow of forty-two !"[1] She was to a marked degree mindful of the contrast between the present and the past—not just giving way to morbid feelings (though certainly she indulged these) but savouring the change, at times with a tinge of indignation that such revolutions should have overtaken her. In the last year of her life and of the nineteenth century, when she was at Osborne in high summer, she remembered that it was the birthday of the Prince Consort and she recounted the

[1] *Letters*, vol. III, p. 602.

happy birthdays of half a century past: "at the dear, lovely Rosenau" in Coburg, at St. Cloud, "that lovely palace, now gone", with Napoleon III and Eugenie, and his last birthday of all at the Viceregal Lodge in Dublin. "All, all is engraven on my mind and in my heart!" she added.[2] And although part of her heart and part of her mind were fixed on the past, impelled by a natural sympathy as well as a sense of duty she was able to live in the present and to move with it. In a striking phrase her last Prime Minister, Lord Salisbury, spoke of her as "bridging over that great interval which separates old England from new England".[3] But she was no mere survivor from Georgian times left stranded on the shores of the Victorian age: no relic of the England of John Bull uneasily lamenting that khaki had replaced the red-coat, that there was a good deal of the Argentine mixed with the roast beef of old England or that the posting house and the mail coach had given way to St. Pancras and an express train to the north. If she was born in George III's reign, she was yet every inch a Victorian—not so much resisting change as helping to create it.

The origins of the Queen were not prosperous. Her father Prince Edward, Duke of Kent, was the fourth son of George III: large, bland, Liberal, talkative, he betrayed an unlucky combination of qualities; he was a moralist and a spendthrift. He had married when he was fifty and he died before his daughter was a year old, leaving behind him a long train of creditors. "My poor father", was the queen's invariable form of words in alluding to him. "Simon Pure" was the harsher term coined for him by his eldest brother. Baron Stockmar, the confidential friend of the Royal Family, thought him "calculating".[4] He had married in 1818 Princes Victoire, born a princess of Saxe-Coburg, and the widow of the minor German prince of Leiningen. Their daughter was born on 24 May 1819, and christened Alexandrina Victoria. In childhood she was known as Alexandrina or Drina for short. At the beginning of 1820 the Duke died, and the Duchess—handsome, endowed with good taste, loving but impetuous—was left with the little

[2]*Letters,* Third series, vol. III, p. 585.   [3]House of Lords, 25 January 1901.
[4]*Memoirs of Baron Stockmar*, vol. I, p. 75.

girl and the debts but consoled with the reflection that it was very likely that one day the girl would be Queen of England. She is *"mon existence"* said the Duchess, who never completely mastered the English language. The child was remarkably like her grandfather, the old King George III. Her mother and an admiring circle of aunts said that the little Princess was *"le roi Georges"* in petticoats".[5] She remained through life a *petite* and rather feminine edition of her grandfather.

The Duchess of Kent was solely responsible for her daughter's upbringing: Parliament appointed her as guardian and Regent if the Princess came to the throne while she was a minor. The Duchess was not liked by the English Royal Family, and this rift meant that the Princess was brought up to a marked degree in isolation from her father's family. She has told us herself that as a girl she invariably screamed when she saw her uncle the Duke of Sussex—possibly because she was alarmed by his black skull-cap. She very seldom saw her uncle George IV and, describing a drive which she took with him in Windsor Great Park, she says, "Mama was much frightened." Her ignorance of her own family—"the old Royal Family" as its members sometimes called it with pride—was complete. Much of her knowledge about the character and habits of her grandparents, uncles and aunts was derived from those long, amusing after-dinner talks with Melbourne after she came to the throne: "Talked of the Princess Sophia Matilda; of the Duke of Gloucester being so exceedingly obstinate: of the obstinacy in the family: George IV was not obstinate, Lord M. said."[6] On the other hand the Queen's relationship to her mother's family was close and natural. When she was seventeen she wrote to her mother's brother, King Leopold, of her unbounded love for him: "it is innate in me, for from my earliest years the name of *Uncle* was the dearest I know, the word *Uncle*, alone, meant no other but you"[7]

The seclusion of the Princess's early years was not diminished by being spent in Kensington. "My dear native town" was the Queen's description in later life of this district of Lon-

[5]*Letters of Harriet Countess Granville*, vol. 1, p. 169.
[6]*Girlhood*, vol. 11, p. 114.   [7]*Letters*, vol. 1, p. 69.

don. And in the 1820's and 1830's Kensington was an entity
detached from the metropolis with many delightful villas, standing in their own gardens, of which the Palace, where the Princess lived, was only a larger and more splendid example. There
was a country air about Kensington, an independence almost
from London which gave it charm, and seemed to protect the
Duchess and her child from the bitter squabbles over the emancipation of the Catholics, the reform of Parliament or the
supposedly swollen emoluments of the gaitered clergy which
agitated the minds of people living further east. The royal
borough seemed protected by a certain rural innocence. Leigh
Hunt once met the future Queen, walking hand in hand with
a childhood's friend from the direction of Bayswater across the
Park. She was followed by a large and splendid footman in
scarlet. The scene struck his imagination and he wrote: "It
brought to our mind the warmth of our own juvenile friendships: and made us fancy that she loved everything else that we
had loved in like measure—books, trees, verses, Arabian tales,
and the good mother who helped to make her so affectionate."[8]

Sir Walter Scott was asked to dinner by the Duchess and
was introduced to the Princess when she was still a girl. Even
at that cursory meeting he noticed that the Duchess and the
governess[9] looked after her exceptionally closely: in fact they
protected her from all outside danger and influence as though
she were the offspring of a golden eagle in its eyrie. On the
whole she was well grounded by tutors, but were isolation
and seclusion the best training-ground for a life destined to be
spent among an almost infinite diversity of people?

The accession of Queen Victoria to the throne on 20 June
1837, when she was just eighteen, was received by the British
people with delight. Perhaps better than anything else her own
words catch the prevailing feeling: when she drove in state

[8]Leigh Hunt, *The Old Court Suburb*, vol. II, p. 258.

[9]Baroness Lehzen – a Hanoverian lady employed by the Duke of Kent
to look after the Duchess's daughter by her first marriage. Her father was
a pastor. She lived until 1870 and when the Queen heard of her death she
wrote: "She had devoted her life to me from my fifth to my eighteenth
year, with the most wonderful self-abnegation, never even taking a day's
leave. I adore her." *Letters*, Second series, vol. II, p. 64.

to the City, five months after her accession, she wrote in her journal: "I met with the MOST gratifying, affectionate, hearty and brilliant reception ... all loyalty, affection and loud greeting."[10] Even by what might be called the hardbitten politicians she was no less well received. A former Prime Minister (Grey) cried with pleasure when he heard her speak, and a Whig Member of Parliament, Creevey, who did not pay idle compliments, wrote: "Our dear little Queen in every respect is *perfection*."[11] Charles Greville, an observer of the political scene and also a severe commentator wrote in his diary: "There was never anything like the first impression she produced or the chorus of praise and admiration which is raised about her manner and behaviour."[12]

Youth of course helped her. For many years the country had had an old Royal Family. Indeed the historian would have to go back to the 1780's, when the princes and princesses of George III's family were at the dawn of their noisy youth, for a time when age was not predominant in the family. As observers watched the first Privy Council of the young Queen, when her two elderly uncles, one in a skull cap, did homage to their niece they sensed the passing of the old generation and the arrival of the new. This realisation of change, of something new, of something young stirred public interest in the monarchy and surrounded it with good-will. On that promising foundation the pose, the simple bearing of the Queen and her obvious goodness raised the monarchy to a pitch of popular favour which it had not enjoyed under the Hanoverian dynasty.

We see her in those early days not only winning the cheers and huzzahs of the crowd but charming the more critical and intimate circle, which was made up of her courtiers, her ministers and the aristocracy. From her first court function when she appeared in black, wearing the insignia of the Garter with blue ribbon, star and a band, bearing the motto, which she wore on her left arm, she showed that she realised a fact—not always appreciated by ladies of the Royal Family—that pageantry is enhanced by a background of black. And on this occasion she

[10]*Girlhood of Queen Victoria*, edited by Lord Fisher, vol. i, pp. 233–5.
[11]Creevey, vol. ii, p. 322.   [12]Greville, vol. iii, p. 372.

demonstrated that she had a knowledge of what to do, together
with a natural diffidence which in combination were irresistible.
She was instinctively considerate to older people: the celebrated
occasion when Lord Rolle stumbled at her Coronation and she
got down from the throne to help him is matched by a less
familiar anecdote about her uncle the Duke of Sussex. Accompanied by certain Fellows of the Royal Society he was received
in private audience by the Queen: as was customary he was
about to kneel and kiss her hand: she immediately stopped him,
rose, put her arm round his neck and touched the hearts of all
the learned gentlemen present by kissing him on the cheek.[13]

About these very early years of Queen Victoria's reign the
enquirer becomes conscious of an air of springlike gaiety which
is almost idyllic. At the end of the first summer of her reign
she wrote in her diary that it was "the pleasantest summer I
EVER passed in *my life*".[14] And the personality of the Queen
slowly glows into life as we glance through the almost artless
prattle of her journal; the reader feels himself slipping into
that long vanished world—watching the Queen, with a degree
of self-importance, struggling through official papers, seeing
her ride out into the Park at Windsor on Leopold or Tartar,
the Prime Minister jogging next her and a cavalcade of the
courtiers with them, or clattering out from Buckingham Palace
for a ride up to north London and past the new cemetery at
Kensal Green: on a wet day playing at battledore and shuttle-
cock, and in the evening learning chess with the Queen of the
Belgians and laughing at the confusion over the Queens playing
and the two Queens on the board: or talking with Melbourne,
her pet dog Islay snoring at her feet, and Melbourne vexing
her by saying that he was a very dull dog. She moved at the
centre of a very brilliant Court, all chosen from the higher
aristocracy—not perhaps of intellectual eminence but accomplished, gay and devoted. The English Court, as King Leopold
once pointed out, was pre-eminent in Europe for brilliance and
elegance. What young girl could fail to be exhilarated at being
the centre of such attention and loyalty? The subtle relationship

[13]Clark and Hughes, *Life and Letters of Adam Sedgwick*, vol. 1, p. 511.
[14]*Girlhood*, vol. 1, p. 229.

between herself and Melbourne when admiration and gratitude deepened into affection can be very clearly traced from the journal. Through her pen we hear the old Whig aristocrat burbling away and passing on to her something of the wisdom and outlook of the eighteenth century. We see them, after dinner at Windsor, looking through the splendid collection of drawings collected by King George IV ("some were not quite eligible and were tacked together") and of his comforting her with the assurance that Virgil was a very difficult author: on another evening he explained to her that he never went to church because he was afraid of hearing something very extraordinary: and then when they were discussing trees he made her jump by suddenly asking, "What's the use of shade in this country?": and (very different from Disraeli's sloppy flattery) he gave it as his opinion that no woman should touch pen and ink because "they have too much passion and too little sense": and when they were discussing burials in Venice he told her that he was not "well acquainted with the dead. *I* like what is joyous and agreeable."

Indeed he liked such things only too well. He seems to have wished to create the Queen and her Court into a kind of stainless Camelot where high ideals were cherished—unsullied by the noisy vitality of a thriving, industrial nation. Certainly it would be unfair to Melbourne to suggest that he wished to exclude from this paradise all the serious side of sovereignty. He encouraged the Queen to work on official business, patiently explaining points of difficulty to her. "He read to me a paper about the Civil List and explained it to me, and so *clearly* and *well* he explained it." But the idea that she should question the wisdom of a particular point of policy or that she might have an individual contribution to make towards Government never crossed his mind. Disagreeable matters like that were for Downing Street or St. Stephen's, she had only to understand and consent. There was truth in the gibe that she was Queen of the Whigs not the Queen of England. For all the brilliance, for all the elegance, for all the idyllic charm of an evening at Windsor and for all its good in developing the Queen and giving her confidence, the influence of Melbourne and her

courtiers were steering the Queen towards disaster; the politician and her friends were creating something remote from
reality, vulnerable to inevitable storms. These, which had been
long brewing, burst with roarings and revealing flashes
shortly before the Queen had been two years on the throne.

The storms threatened from two quarters. The first was
political. Melbourne's Government was weak. Not only were
some of his cabinet colleagues of doubtful capacity but both
in Lords and Commons his majority was frail. In the Commons
the Liberal or Radical members were always liable to desert
him in a critical division, and he really owed his existence to
Irish support and to the Conservative feeling that their party
was as yet hardly strong enough to form a government on
their own. These political trepidations tinge the Queen's
journal time and time again: the following extract from 7 March
1838 is typical: "He [Lord Melbourne] said, 'I am not quite
so sure of to-night; I think we shall carry it, but you must not
be surprised if it should be the other way . . .' tears were nearer
than words to me at that moment. . . ."[15] The danger was that
the tears would be realised outside the Palace and that the
public would identify the Queen too closely with the Whigs.
"Vote for McDruggy and our young Queen" recalls Disraeli
in Sybil with the Tory riposte: "We issued our placard
instantly of 'Vote for our young Queen and Egremont', which
was at least more modest and turned out more popular."

The other quarter from which the storm threatened lay in
the jealousies and rivalries within the palace itself. But in order
to understand how they came about, the reader needs to
be apprised of events earlier in the Queen's life, and to step
back from the brilliant gaieties of Buckingham Palace to the
secluded dullness of Kensington. For in Kensington Palace lay
the origins of what is known to history as the Bedchamber
Plot.

The Duchess of Kent was not unreasonably conscious of the
responsibility of being the sole custodian of the heiress to the
throne, and she was also (likewise with reason) proud of
the efficiency with which she discharged that responsibility. She

[15]*Girlhood*, vol. 1, p. 293.

once made reference in public to "the undoubted confidence placed in me by the country, being the only parent since the Restoration who has had the uncontrolled power in bringing up the heir to the throne". If King William died before Princess Victoria was eighteen, the Duchess would have been Regent. The prospect was tantalising. If she was Regent, she would be able to reward with place and pension those faithful retainers of the Duke of Kent who had clung to her, with devotion, through the dead years of widowhood. Such was the Duchess's hope—at once understandable and laudable—in fact the legitimate aspiration of every trustee who has given care and time to a bankrupt estate, and wishes to gratify himself by the feel of power as wealth begins to pour into the trust.

With the dawn of 1837 it became clear that the race between the old King's death and the young girl's majority was to be in the words of the Duke of Wellington on another occasion "a damn'd near-run thing". At once there was a flurry in Kensington Palace—a purposeful bustle about the Duchess and her retinue—not unlike the scurry of ants as light breaks in on their habitation. Learned men have pondered whether ants, in their roamings, are moved by reason, and we may, in turn be forgiven for wondering whether reason governed the Duchess, her principal adviser Sir John Conroy[16] and the ladies of her exclusive little court.[17] Although the intrigues and ambitions within Kensington Palace obtrude themselves with hint and innuendo into the history books they have seemingly never received a close inspection. (On this topic the Queen was naturally extremely reserved.) But they deserve to be observed with the unflinching gaze of the naturalist through his glass. This much is clear. The Duchess was certainly unwise—although we need not endorse Creevey's verdict that she was "the most restless, persevering, troublesome devil possible".[18] She acquiesced in a plot of Conroy and Lady Flora that if her daughter

[16]He was an Irish soldier of great ambition who had been in the service of the Duke of Kent.

[17]Lady Flora Hastings, daughter of a former Governor-General of Bengal, was the lady of the court most in the confidence of the Duchess.

[18]*Creevey's Life and Times*, edited by John Gore, p. 372.

won the race and became eighteen before King William breathed his last, they would press her to agree to a Regency—even though she was in fact of age—because of her youth and inexperience. For Conroy the prize glittered temptingly and close at hand: it would be too cruel to lose it: he therefore went further than the ladies and urged that the Princess must be forced to agree to a Regency, if she would not do so of her own accord. Then began a systematic ill-treatment of the girl by Conroy and Lady Flora—she was taunted with being stupid, with being mean like her grand-mother Queen Charlotte, and with looking like her uncle the Duke of Gloucester who, in profile, resembled the head of a splended cod lying on the fishmonger's slab. (He was affectionately known as "slice".) They whispered outside: the Princess was sullen and stupid: she knew of her imperfections: she herself wished for a Regency. The Cabinet caught wind of what was being said: Whig lords arriving at Kensington, listened, lowered their tones and reported back to Downing Street.

Perhaps the Queen could have saved herself—but she was young. In fact she was rescued by three people. Stockmar,[19] Baroness Lehzen and Melbourne, and this fact explains her singular devotion to all three. The first two had no difficulty in establishing that the Princess was by no means stupid, and that she had no desire for a Regency. She herself, as she confessed later, was intensely unhappy but she never enlarged on these troubles; and if they were referred to in her Journal, such references were discreetly omitted by her editors. In Stockmar's Memoirs, which were published during the Queen's lifetime, there is merely a veiled allusion to "great and unwonted difficulties" followed by the bald statement that Stockmar rendered her "essential services at this critical juncture".[20]

Some might be disposed to think that these palace squabbles are the commonplaces of courts, and merit scant attention. But

[19]Baron Stockmar was originally Prince Leopold's doctor. He subsequently became the shrewd and devoted adviser of the whole Coburg family.

[20]Memoirs of Baron Stockmar, vol. i, p. 377. Even in later life she made no allusion to what she had endured – no doubt out of loyalty to the memory of her mother.

they help to explain one thing which struck every observer on the 20 June, when the Princess assumed the majesty—namely her composure and self-reliance. She had acquired them in the hardest school.

Moreover, when she came to the throne, the circumstances which gave rise to these palace troubles were not changed: the Duchess and her coterie were still at Court: the plotters were not routed, plenty of malice was left in them. The reader will appreciate that when the Queen came to the throne her mother did not move into a separate house.[21] She lived with the Queen at Buckingham Palace and Windsor, accompanied by the same attendants who had been with her at Kensington. Her little posse of devoted adherents was from the start on poor terms with the influential body of courtiers who marshalled by Baroness Lehzen, made up the Queen's Court. In any circumstances these twin courts under one roof were likely to give rise to bickering and tittle-tattle, and when Sir John Conroy, whose Irish familiarities with ladies would have made a good subject for one of Thackeray's sketches, was the chief ingredient of the smaller court trouble was certain. Conroy's most faithful adherent was the Duchess's lady-in-waiting, Lady Flora Hastings, who had become increasingly sharp-tongued and perhaps somewhat unbalanced. In the autumn of 1838 she and Conroy had travelled together from Scotland in a post-chaise, and when news of this excursion reached the larger court the obvious interpretation was placed upon it. Shortly afterwards Lady Flora enlarged in appearance—a fact which, coupled with other symptoms commented upon in whispers by ladies, gave rise to a reasonable belief that she was with child. She was eventually, through pressure of the larger court, forced to agree to a medical examination which revealed—not a pregnancy but mortal illness. Conroy (as may be supposed) was delighted with this promising game and halloo'd on the Duchess and Lady Flora: in particular he agitated Lady Flora until she complained to her family, who speedily paraded their

[21]The Duchess went to Belgrave Square after the Queen's marriage, and in 1842 to Clarence House.

wrongs in the newspapers. The matter was incredibly badly handled, and even making full allowance for the inexperience of the Queen the critics might say that she showed great harshness. Moreover she openly quarrelled with the Duchess—certainly a foolish woman but good-hearted and loving and not easy to treat with harsh snubs.[22] But for all its importance in the history books and scandals of the day the case of Lady Flora is only the second chapter of the rather sordid tale which opened in the peace and quiet of Kensington Palace.

Some might argue, as did the diarist Greville, that this skeleton is scarcely worth resurrecting since it merely shows that *"les Rois et les valets"* are made of the refuse clay of creation. Yet the case of Flora Hastings is important partly because it reflects the less agreeable (and less familiar) side of the Queen's character and chiefly because the Bedchamber Question is unintelligible without knowing this background. When the Flora Hastings hubbub was at its height the Tory newspapers and Tory ladies—and the latter are often the more redoubtable of the two—howled aloud their abuse of the Court and implied that the trouble had only arisen because the Queen had surrounded herself with Whig ladies and nothing but Whig ladies. When the uproar was at its height Melbourne resigned, after his Government had found its majority in the Commons reduced to five; as a condition of taking office, Peel insisted that some of the Whig ladies should resign and Tories take their place. There can be no doubt that the Queen resisted Peel's demands because she saw thereby a chance of saving the Whig Ministry and keeping Melbourne, but also—and this important point is generally overlooked—because she feared that the Tories would sweep out Lehzen, thereby enabling the Duchess of Kent and Conroy to triumph, and give the impression that they were cleaning up a morally corrupt court. Greville,

[22]"Oh! I am so wretched to think *how, for a time, two people most wickedly estranged us . . . it drives me wild now."* So wrote the Queen after her mother's death in 1861, *Letters,* vol. III, p. 560. All the papers dealing with this tangled question are believed to have been burned by King Edward when he came to the throne. When he read them he was astonished at the precocious knowledge shown by the Queen.

who was well informed on this, says that Peel suggested the
necessity for changes in the ladies "for reasons (especially taken
with other things) by no means insufficient".

Having overcome the first shock—when she was told by
Lord John Russell that the cabinet had decided to resign and
was given the reasons therefore, she was throughout the interview dissolved in tears—she played her difficult hand with
nerve and spirit. Peel told her that if he was to attempt to
form a government he would need evidence of the Queen's confidence, and that could only be given by dismissing some of
her Whig ladies and filling their places with supporters of the
Tory Government. This the Queen flatly refused.[23] For a girl
of twenty the plight was grievous: she did allow herself to indulge in a rather girlish sneer that the ladies seemed to be Sir
Robert's only support, and she wept copiously after her inter-
views with the Tory leaders, but there is no reason to doubt
her own description of herself as "being very much collected
civil and high". To Melbourne she wrote: "The Queen of
England will not submit to such trickery."

Peel threw in his hand: Melbourne and his Whig colleagues
returned to office, survived for two years and perhaps events
justified the Queen's political acumen, for it could be argued
that Peel's support was too feeble to offer any chance of per-
manence. The whole episode shows the strength of the Queen's
character, and a certain hardness which, even in her youth,
she could assume with great effect. As Creevey, with familiarity,
expressed it: "the Queen is a resolute little tit."[24] Not for nothing
was she daughter to that harsh disciplinarian, the Duke of
Kent, of whom a private soldier remarked thirty years after
his death, "I recollect him well. He was a very bad man.
He would not let us drink." Like her father, the Queen showed

[23]From the constitutional point of view there was some ambiguity. Court
ladies had not previously changed with the Government, though the
leading male members of the Court had. Peel got round this by arguing
that the ladies in former reigns had not changed because they were attached
to a Queen Consort: the case – he maintained – was altered with a Queen
Regnant since her ladies, to an extent, took the place of men attached to
a male sovereign.
[24]Creevey, vol. II, p. 324.

that the servant of an institution, whether the Army or the monarchy, must have something more than affability and vapid graciousness. She inherited the tradition—and her personality did not weaken it—that the sovereign should, on occasions, show displeasure. The governments of the Hanoverians expected the Head of the State to mark with recognisable disapproval those who were lax supporters or open critics. When Lord Lyndhurst, a Whig renegade, attended her first levée she was described as "drawing herself up as if she had seen a snake".[25] Although the Queen in these opening years of her reign has been generally drawn in the gentlest colours—the innocent maid moving with acclaim among the survivors of the full-blooded life of Regency England—that was only part of the picture. We should neither do justice to the robustness of her character nor account for those sterner streaks in her, which became more conspicuous with age, if their presence was slurred over in the days of her youth. Sixty years later she told her secretary that she was very young at the time of the Bedchamber Plot, "perhaps I should act differently if it were all to be done again". That we may respectfully but decidedly beg leave to doubt.

II

As we listen to the Queen unfolding her private feelings in her talks with Melbourne ("a man in whom I can safely place confidence")[26] or read her, when she has committed her inmost thought to the privacy of her journal, we realise how completely normal, straightforward and uninhibited she was. To the twentieth century, tortured by extravagant fancies on the human passions, the simplicity of romance in the middle years of the nineteenth century is at once affecting and incomprehensible. When the Queen's heart was touched she at once confessed the truth without reserve and without relish: every page of her journal reveals her admiration for Melbourne hardening into affection till looking back on things from the vantage point of a happy marriage she confessed her romantic attachment to him; she wrote in her diary that "my unbounded affection and admiration for Lord Melbourne... arose from the fact that I clung to someone and having very warm feelings".[27] When the future Emperor Alexander II of Russia visited this country as Czarevitch (and gave his name to a famous race at New-market), the Queen wrote in her journal, on saying "good-bye", "I felt so sad to take leave of this dear amiable young man, whom I really think (talking jokingly) I was a little in love with. . . ."[28]

The Duchess of Kent and her brother King Leopold had a long-standing ambition that the Queen should marry their nephew Albert, the younger of the two sons of their eldest brother, the reigning Duke of Saxe-Coburg. He was lively, very clever and exceptionally good-looking—though like most members of the Coburg family he was marked by melancholy, and his spirits were languid. As early as the summer of 1836, when she was seventeen, the Queen had developed warm feel-ings for the Prince and, after his visit to Kensington Palace in that year, she had written to thank her uncle for "the prospect of *great* happiness you have given me in the person of dear Albert".[29] But unfortunately the excitements of her acces-sion and the gaieties of her Court banished thoughts of Albert with "his pleasing and delightful exterior" from her mind. The image faded. He wrote: she did not reply. But within two years the difficulties which the Queen encountered over the Bedchamber question and Lady Flora and her consequent loss of popularity determined her uncle Leopold to revive the Coburg marriage. Her other uncle, the Prince's father, was also determined that his son should not be kept dangling, left perhaps till he was in his early twenties and then dismissed from his suit with no prospects, no money and no bride. He had no intention that his son should play the role of the Duc d'-Alençon to this nineteenth-century Queen Elizabeth. In July 1839 the Queen unburdened herself in a private letter to her uncle sent for safety by a courier. She first of all wished the

[27]*Journal*, quoted in *The Prince Consort*, by Roger Fulford, p. 42.
[28]*Girlhood*, vol. II, p. 191.   [29]*Letters*, vol. I, p. 62.

family to know that there was no understanding about an engagement between the Prince and herself. If he came on a visit to England, she could make no final promise that year, and in any event there could be no question of any marriage for two or three years. She asserted that there was *"no anxiety"* in the country for her marriage.[30] She added that she was nervous about her cousin's visit, and that the subject was not an agreeable one.[31] A more damping letter for the match-maker in Brussels it is difficult to conceive. Whether the contents of this letter were passed on to the suitor is difficult to say: he seemingly knew that she might put off the whole project for some years because he said to her, in later life, that he came to England with the intention of telling her that if she could not make up her mind he would not wait for three or four years. But when in October 1839 the young Prince, who was just twenty, arrived at Windsor, with his elder brother, the artificial delights of Lord Melbourne's talk and the vanities of court life were gathered into oblivion like the dreams and nightmares of sleep in the clear light of dawn. The tone of her letters to her uncle abruptly changes as "the dear cousins" arrived on 10 October. Albert's "beauty" is striking: the cousins are amiable: they are passionately fond of music, and "are playing a Haydn symphony as I write", till on 15 October she writes of *"perfection"*, and announces her engagement, With that frankness which never deserted her, and a realisation that, in spite of a very determined nature, she could be wrong, she added: "My feelings are a *little* changed, I must say, since last Spring, when I said I couldn't *think* of marrying for *three* or *four* years; but seeing Albert has changed all this."[32]

Should we picture Prince Albert as a pawn moved forward to confront the Queen by the acumen of his ambitious uncle, but with little more inclination for the task than the heartless figure on the chess-board? To the twentieth-century mind there

[30]This is rather curious, because if the Queen had died or had no children the crown would have passed to her uncle, the King of Hanover, possibly the most unpopular member of the Royal Family in our annals. Her marriage was the most effectual bar to his succession.

[31]*Letters*, vol. i, p. 223.   [32]*Ibid.*, vol. i, p. 239.

is something distasteful about a marriage planned by family
advisers, yet such arranged marriages were in reality often more
durable, happier and more loving than those springing from
an untrammelled choice. The Queen was demonstrative: the
Prince was not. The Queen was high spirited and gay: the
Prince was low spirited and serious. Yet their marriage was
among the happiest and most successful in the history of the
English Royal Family. Whether its success arose from necessity,
from companionship or from love is not easily answered by
those who never saw them together. We can only say that
through a married life of twenty-one years, in which they
produced nine children, they remained in 1861 as devoted as
they were in 1840 and wished for no greater happiness than
the enjoyment of each other's company in seclusion.[33]

But seclusion, attainable by ordinary mortals as easily as
bread or light or water, was denied to the owner of Buckingham Palace or Windsor Castle. The marriage took place in the
Chapel Royal at St. James's Palace on 10 February 1840. Al-
thought convenient, when two or three are gathered together,
the Chapel is small so that the Queen escaped the tedium of
a modern royal wedding where Westminster Abbey is crammed
with tier upon tier of official bores. These were accommodated in
1840 within the Palace but outside the chapel, in stands and
boxes erected for the day. They quickly succeeded in trans-
forming a religious occasion into a raree-show, rising in their
seats to cheer and flutter lace-frilled handkerchiefs when famous
persons moved into the chapel, reserving their most spirited
manifestations for the bridegroom. The Prince wore the uniform of a British field-marshal, but his pale and pensive good
looks were emphasised by a bible, bound in green velvet, which
he carried instead of the customary baton.[34] After the wedding
breakfast at Buckingham Palace the Queen and Prince drove
to Windsor, where they were given an uproarious welcome by

[33]Immediately after the Prince's death the Queen's eldest daughter,
who was staying with her, wrote: "Mama had so desperately longed for
another child." As was true of King George III and Queen Charlotte,
the love of the parents for the younger members of their large family
was in contrast to their feelings for the elder sons.

[34]Annual Register, 1840.

the loyal citizens and the Eton boys, and where they stayed for five days.

The Prince had wished to stay down in Windsor quietly for some days, but the Queen assured him: "I must come out after the second day."[35] Her authority for this was the opinion of her aged aunts, who were citing what had happened when their father, King George III, had married threequarters of a century before. Yet the far-sighted members of the Court had the chance to notice one portent which suggested that the imperious young Queen of twenty was not always to be the dominant member of the two. On the morning following their wedding the bride and bridegroom were detected out walking early in the morning. "That's not the way to provide us with a Prince of Wales," gloomily observed the diarist Greville.[36] This blunt remark skirted over the point of interest—namely the change in the Queen's habits. Before marriage she was always a late riser and generally sat down to her breakfast about 10 o'clock. The Prince on the other hand loathed late nights— even as a youth he always found difficulty in keeping awake at an evening party—but he loved to be out in the early morning observing natural life and listening to the song of birds. At this time the Queen was essentially a Londoner ("I am never easy if I am not on the spot," she once told him),[37] the Prince on the other hand was a countryman, inspired by the romantic countryside of southern Germany before the arrival of industrialism. Here then is the first triumph of the Prince: he led the Queen away from urban delights, from con stantly hungering after company to the joy of a self-con tained home life. Like all people who have had a short, per functory courtship the Queen was perhaps nervous at first of being cooped up with a man whom she really scarcely knew Her cousin Princess Charlotte, who married the Queen's uncle Leopold, wrote to a friend two days after marriage: "I can not say that I feel much at my ease or quite comfortable ye. in his society, but it will wear away, I dare say, this sort of

[35]Quoted in Roger Fulford, *The Prince Consort*.
[36]*Greville Memoirs*, vol. IV, p. 241.
[37]R. Fulford, p. 50. *The Prince Consort*.

awkwardness."[38] No doubt the Queen had feelings which were not dissimilar. For posterity the interest of the Queen's marriage, as it developed, lies in the gradual emergence of a home behind the frontage of the Court, of a private life behind the façade of her public life.

For the first two and a half years of her reign—the years when she was Queen but unmarried—her private life was bounded by the Court. Her relations with her mother had become purely formal. Her relaxation was in talk with Melbourne, in the enjoyment of the society of her rather gay and dashing Court and (it has to be said) of a good deal of tittle-tattle about personalities. The celebrated dictum of good breeding, that gentlefolk talk about things while servants talk about people, certainly did not govern the conversation at the Queen's Court. Turning to the Queen's *Journal* we find ourselves translated into a delightful world of small talk—something between a country house in Edwardian times and the senior commonroom of an Oxford College. Riding in Windsor Park the Queen discussed the marriage of the Belgian Minister to the daughter of Joshua Bates—an American who was senior partner in Baring's—"a great match in point of money which Lord Palmerston said was a great thing".[39] Lady Lyttelton asked if she might wear glasses to do her needlework, and Melbourne at once told the Queen that this proved that she understood etiquette, since in George III's day spectacles were banned at Court.[40] She and Melbourne discussed the passionate love of a youth for Lady Ashley—wife of the philanthropist who was later Lord Shaftesbury. "It often wears off, but it kills others," Lord Melbourne told her.[41] When the Queen and Melbourne were discussing perfumes he told her that Lady Holland always insisted on her servants taking away people's pockethandkerchiefs if they had any scent on them.[42] The Queen was also regaled with the fact that Lady Holland particularly disliked William IV's bastard daughter who had married her

[38]*The Letters of The Princess Charlotte*, edited by Professor Arthur Aspinall, 1949, p. 243.

[39]*Journal*, vol. II, p. 15.   [40]*Ibid.*, vol. II, p. 41.
[41]*Ibid.*, vol. II, p. 49.   [42]*Ibid.*, vol. II, p. 62.

illegitimate son, Charles Fox.[43] And on the same family the Queen was diverted with the information that Charles James Fox's widow, who was over ninety, had had a tooth drawn which was perfectly sound.[44] And later: "Talked of Lord Douro's marriage to one of Lord Tweeddale's daughters: both Lady Normanby and I said we should not believe it till we saw Lord Douro really married because he was so very changeable: they said Lord Douro had been out shopping with the young lady. And Lord M said, 'shopping is very demonstrative'."[45] On another occasion they talked of Peel's unpopularity: "A very bad manner, a very disagreeable *abord*," was Melbourne's comment.[46] And they chattered away about the boy who stole at Eton, of Lord Anglesey's children by his second marriage who all took after their mother, of the Duchess of Sutherland, who grumbled because she had only £12,000 a year, of Lady Wilhelmina Stanhope's long face, and of Lord Westminster at the age of seventy-two dancing with the Duchess of Somerset.

In fairness to the young Queen, the reader will notice that these free and easy comments on people were exchanged with Melbourne—or always when he was present and the centre of conversation. Though she enjoyed the companionship of her courtiers she was reserved with them. She once asked Melbourne whether she was rumoured to show preferences for any of her courtiers. Melbourne assured her that she did not, complimented her and added that: "it was strange for so young a person not to show any preference". The Queen added: "I dared not." But although she might reveal no partialities, her private happiness and her private life were divided between Melbourne and the company of her courtiers. Though there was nothing reprehensible in this, it was for a girl an existence which was strange and unnatural. From this her marriage rescued her— a fact of which she was quickly conscious. When she re-read her *Journal* in 1842 she added this very significant comment: "I cannot forbear remarking what an artificial sort of happiness *mine* was *then*, and what a blessing it is I have now in

[43]*Ibid.*, vol. II, p. 74. [44]*Ibid.*, vol. II, p. 231.
[45]*Ibid.*, vol. II, p. 123. [46]*Ibid.*, vol. II, p. 150.

my beloved husband, *real* and solid happiness ... it was but in Society that I had amusement, and I was only living on that superficial resource, which I *then fancied* was happiness."[47]

Well may the reader wonder how the youth of twenty achieved this palace revolution—this transformation in the character of the Queen. (And it will not be overlooked that Queen Victoria, throughout life, took some pleasure in proclaiming her obstinacy. Her temper also was quick, a lack of control which she also admitted. In writing to her half-sister, Princess Feodore, she asked whether they had not both inherited their sharp tempers from their grandmother—the Dowager Duchess of Coburg.) In explaining how this change was brought about, we should certainly give pride of place to the Queen's rapidly growing adoration of the Prince. For the shrewdness and wisdom of this young man, not yet of age, was a conspicuous reason for his influence over the Queen. He might so easily by rushing into the *tracasseries* of the Court, by taking up the cudgels on behalf of his aunt, the Duchess of Kent, or by trying to tear asunder the Queen's Whig bias, have involved himself in fatal difficulties which would have destroyed the Queen's confidence in him. His immediate triumph, in the first year of his marriage, was to restore the affectionate relationship between the Queen and her mother. When the Queen came to see how silly and uncomfortable the squabble had been, she must have been impressed by the Prince's good sense and tact. His next achievement was to prepare the ground for the inevitable break with Melbourne, when the Whig Government collapsed—an event which happened in the autumn of 1841. When Melbourne finally quitted the service of the Queen—an occasion marked by tears from the Queen and deep emotion from the statesman—he detailed with praise the Prince's gifts. "I am so glad to hear Lord M say this. Perhaps this may be a good lesson for me."[48] We may assume that she meant by this that it was a lesson to teach her to rely less on her own feelings and more on the Prince's judgement and discretion.

The fall of Melbourne left unprotected the gay Court of the Queen's early years. Its inmates were chosen largely for their bearing, birth and good looks: most of them were descended from the famous cavalry officer—one of the most dazzling men of his time—Lord Anglesey or those who had intermarried with his relations. The Paget family (to give them their patronymic) eschewed from life all that was sombre or tedious: they shone with lustre in an atmosphere of sparkle and brilliance. "The Paget system is never to learn anything," said Lord Melbourne. They were invariably smart: George IV, conscious of his own unwieldy figure, once plaintively asked his tailor: "Why don't you make my coats fit like Paget's?" It would be wrong to imply that there was anything immoral or indecorous about the Queen's Court: rather it resembled White's Club on a quiet day, when the observer feels that all are on their best behaviour but is yet conscious of smouldering fires of roystering passion which could blaze up at any moment.

The link between the Queen and her courtiers—that is to say the person who made the necessary arrangements for any festivities or the turns of waiting—was the rather unexpected figure of her former governess—the Hanoverian Baroness Lehzen. "That most dear Being" was the description given of her by the Queen.[49] But "my most dearly beloved angelic Lehzen", for ever sucking caraway seeds—a carminative greatly beloved by her generation as a means of expelling wind— was a complete barrier against the Prince's influence within the home. "I am only the husband and not the master in the house," wrote the Prince to one of his closest friends.[50]

When the complications of a nursery[51] had to be imposed

[49]*Letters*, vol. 1, p. 156.   [50]Martin, vol. 1, p. 71.
[51]The following were the children of the Queen and Prince:

1. Victoria Adelaide Mary Louisa, born 21 November 1840, married 25 January 1858 Prince Frederick of Prussia, died 5 August 1901. Princess Royal, Empress of Germany.

2. Albert Edward, born 9 November 1841, married 10 March 1863 Princess Alexandra of Denmark, died 6 May 1910. Prince of Wales, King Edward VII.

3. Alice Maud Mary, born 25 April 1843, married 1 July 1862 Prince Louis of Hesse, died 14 December 1878. Grand Duchess of Hesse-Darmstadt.

4. Alfred Ernest Albert, born 6 August 1844, married 23 January 1874 Grand-Duchess Marie of Russia, died 30 July 1900. Duke of Edinburgh and reigning Duke of Saxe-Coburg and Gotha.

on the Court the Baroness not unnaturally expected to have as much control over that establishment as she had over the hairdressers, the wardrobe women and the bedchamber women. She had some sharp encounters with the Prince, and she perhaps showed her wisdom in not attempting to stand her ground, but withdrew to Germany exactly a year after the fall of Melbourne. A year before she went, the Prince, in private conversation with Melbourne, had told him that the interference of the Baroness "kept him in a constant state of annoyance". The two men agreed that it would not be possible to remove the Baroness "without an exciting scene with the Queen" and that it was best to leave such things to time. The diplomacy needed by her advisers, by Melbourne and by the Prince before they dared tackle this thorny problem reveals, with the frankness of a mirror, the difficult streak which ran through the Queen's character. She was by nature obstinate and self-willed, and when loyalty to persons was imposed on those qualities she became intractable. No event shows more clearly than the gradual eclipse of the Baroness how completely the Prince was taking possession of the Queen's heart.

But perhaps the Prince has not been given sufficient credit for one matter by posterity. Although his control over the Queen

---

5. Helena Augusta Victoria, born 25 May 1846, married 5 July 1866 Prince Christian of Schleswig-Holstein, died 9 June 1923. Princess Christian.
6. Louise Caroline Alberta, born 18 March 1848, married 21 March 1871 Marquis of Lorne, died 3 December 1939. Princess Louise, Duchess of Argyll.
7. Arthur William Patrick Albert, born 1 May 1850, married 13 March 1879 Princess Louise of Prussia, died 16 January 1942. Duke of Connaught.
8. Leopold George Duncan Albert, born 7 April 1853, married 27 April 1882 Princess Helen of Waldeck, died 28 March 1884. Duke of Albany.
9. Beatrice Mary Victoria Feodore, born 14 April 1857, married 23 July 1885 Prince Henry of Battenburg, died 26 October 1944. Princess Beatrice.
    The Queen's and Prince's choice of christian names is in keeping with the attachment to mediaeval times which characterised the nineteenth century. Queen Victoria herself liked "old English names". She did not like the name George and here again her break with the Hanoverian dynasty was marked. The name of Charlotte was not perpetuated, nor the fine name Augustus, which had been carried by almost all the English princes of the Queen's family – including her father.

became dominant he never used it merely to get his own way, but reserved it for those issues on which he felt that the well-being of the Queen or the monarchy was at stake. For example he very quickly became bored by the tittle-tattle of an evening at Court, by the long-drawn games of chess or even the excitements of a game of cards called The Yellow Dwarf. He wished to bring literary and scientific people about the Court, to vary the society and make it a more general reflection of English life.[52] The Queen, however, felt that she would not have been at ease in such company, and it was completely foreign to her straightforward nature to pretend to understand matters of which she had no knowledge. On this, which was merely a matter of his own preference, the Prince did not attempt to force his own wishes.

The most far-reaching of the changes effected by the Prince on the Queen's habit of life was to withdraw her from social life into the home. Perhaps the extent of this has hardly been appreciated, but it paved the way for—and partially explains—the immuring of herself after his death into the homes which they had created. They inherited establishments which were created for an earlier tradition of monarchy. Buckingham Palace, enormous but central, was the business headquarters of the monarchy without accommodation for a family or the paraphernalia of children, and exposed to the searching eye of everybody passing through that central point of the capital. Windsor was more secluded—yet on one side private houses were clustered all round it both inside and outside the walls. The Pavalion at Brighton—that gem of oriental taste—was like a small oasis in a modern new town. Lodging houses and marine resorts hemmed it in on every side so that the Queen complained that she could not stir out of doors without being mobbed. Writing to one of her aunts in 1845—the last year in which she stayed at the Pavilion—the Queen wrote: "the people are very indiscreet and troublesome here really, which makes this place quite a prison".[53] In fact a perceptible change was develop-

[52]*Letters*, vol. 1, p. 322.
[53]Quoted in Clifford Musgrave, *Royal Pavilion. A Study in the Romantic*, 1951.

ing in the attitude of British people towards their sovereign. Sixty years earlier George III at Windsor used to call on friends inside and outside the precincts of the castle with no warning except the thunderous rat-tat-tat of a royal servant. Anyone within the house, except the person whom the King had come to see, withdrew themselves as far as they could from royal notice, falling back to the wall as the King came in. But in Queen Victoria's reign falling back was giving way to pressing forwards. Curiosity was mastering good manners. This was particularly noticeable at Brighton. When the Prince Regent first went to Brighton he was treated with the greatest respect: in fact a majority of the residents and visitors were his acquaintances or friends. At that time there were just over 1,000 occupied houses: by Queen Victoria's time the number had increased seven-fold. The growth of population, its mobility (the railway to Brighton was opened in 1841) and a determination to see and stare—people were supposed to have pressed right up to the Queen and peered under her poke-bonnet—introduced a new and formidable problem. Both the Prince and the Queen were determined to find a home removed from the great centres of population. They were able to buy an attractive property, Osborne, on the northern tip of the Isle of Wight facing Portsmouth. They stayed there for the first time in 1845 and writing to Lord Melbourne the Queen said she "thinks it is impossible to imagine a prettier spot—valleys and woods which would be beautiful anywhere: but all this near the sea (the woods grow into the sea) is quite perfection: we have a charming beach quite to ourselves ... we can walk about anywhere by ourselves without being followed and mobbed, which Lord Melbourne will easily understand is delightful".[54]

They rebuilt the house, and always contrived to spend some part of the early summer at Osborne, the Queen reading official papers under the garden trees while the Prince worked in the woods, and the children raced round without constraint. There was in truth something idyllic about what the Prince called "our island home".

Yet to one familiar with the beauties of the mountains and

forests of his native land the pastoral scenery of southern England seemed a shade unromantic and trim. The decision to
explore Scotland was the Prince's, but the scenery and the
people satisfied some of the deepest feelings of the Queen.
Soon after they were married they paid two visits to Scotland,
the first in 1842 and the second in 1844. At the end of this
second visit the Queen wrote in her journal: "There is a great
peculiarity about the *Highlands* and Highlanders; and they are
such a chivalrous, fine, active people. Our stay among them
was delightful.

Independently of the beautiful scenery, there was a quiet,
a retirement, a wildness, a liberty and a solitude that had such
charm for us."[55]

They were drawn to Balmoral by the knowledge that it was
drier than in the more picturesque parts of Scotland to the west,
and by the advice of their doctor. They first went to Balmoral in
the summer of the year of Revolution, 1848, taking a lease of
the castle and then buying it four years later. In 1849 they converted and enlarged a cottage some 5 or 6 miles from the castle,
where the Queen and Prince could live in absolute seclusion
amid scenery which the Queen called "solemn and striking".[56]
The castle itself was rebuilt in 1852.

The reader who wishes to gauge the depth of the Queen's
devotion to Scotland must turn to the ample account of her
life there to be found in the *Journal*.[57] And if the enthusiasms of
the Queen are felt at times to be too emphatic we can see them
as they appeared in the summer of 1849 to that crotchety observer of Victorian life, Charles Greville, who prefaced the
account of his stay there with an emphatic allusion to how
much "I dislike Courts and all that appertains to them". But
he had to add that at Balmoral the Queen appeared to great
advantage. "The place is very pretty," he wrote, "the house

[55]*Leaves from the Journal of Our Life in the Highlands*, p. 42.

[56]*Journal of Our Life in the Highlands*, p. 75. After the Prince's death
the Queen could not bear to stay in this Hut or Bothie, as it was called,
and she built another on the edge of Loch Muick.

[57]The reader is also referred to the excellent account of Balmoral in
a book published in 1955 by Mr. Ivor Brown, which effectively brushes
on one side the prickly feelings of Scotsmen about "Balmorality".

very small. They live there without any state whatever: they live not merely like private gentlefolks, but like very small gentlefolks, small house, small rooms, small establishment."[58]

Many—possibly too many—books have been devoted to the charms and delights of Queen Victoria's private life. Yet reflection suggests that such ample notice is not altogether misplaced. The Queen herself would certainly have wished this side of her life to be squarely stated to posterity. Writing to her uncle three years after her marriage she said: "Indeed, dearest Uncle, I will venture to say that not only no *Royal Ménage* is to be found equal to *ours*, but no other *ménage* is to be compared to ours...."[59] From her published correspondence the attentive reader could extract many similarly ecstatic references to her domestic happiness. Writing to her royal uncle the Queen might be accused of some lack of feeling in sweeping on one side the claims of his own *ménage*. But, whatever might have happened if his first wife Princess Charlotte had lived (to whom he always looked back with touching constancy), his second marriage to the daughter of his neighbour, King Louis Philippe, was made for convenience and dynastic reasons. He found her, we may surmise, somewhat languid and boring. The great sovereigns of Europe at this time in Schönbrunn at Vienna, in Versailles, in the Winter Palace at St. Petersburg or at the Escurial in Madrid led lives of dignity but restraint. The plight of the smaller potentates in Holland, Germany and Italy was more noticeable: they could not escape the attention of their bourgeois subjects—a state of affairs amusingly described by King Leopold when he wrote: "Here one is exactly shut up as if one was in a menagerie, walking round and round like a tame bear."[60] Greater freedom and a more retired domestic freedom as they gradually broke loose from the old traditions of etiquette developed later in the nineteenth century for the monarchs of Europe. But we may suspect that one reason for Queen Victoria's exultation lay in the fact that she was conspicuously different in this respect from her fellow-sovereigns and that she

[58]This was of course before the building of the present castle.
[59]*Letters*, vol. I, p. 594.
[60]*Letters*, vol. I, p. 441.

could reasonably claim to be a pioneer in excluding the formality and protocol of a court from her home life.[61] This transformation in the outlook of the Queen was the conspicuous achievement of Prince Albert. The following extracts from her letters show how quickly and completely he converted her. The reader will remember how, just before the wedding, she explained that it was not possible for her to be away from London for more than a few days: "I am never easy a moment, if I am not on the spot."[62] Exactly four years later she was writing to her uncle: "God knows *how willingly* I would *always* live with my beloved Albert and our children in the quiet and retirement of private life."[63]

However, the picture of the Queen would be awry if she was viewed as sacrificing her sense of royal dignity to her love of privacy. The woman who enjoyed running into a crofter's cottage, who was delighted when the owner welcomed her with the words: "Come in, Queen Victoria," was capable of an effortless assumption of royal authority. For she discharged the ceremonial side of the British monarchy with a grace and distinction which won the admiration of her subjects and the envy of foreign observers. Her natural advantages were not conspicuous for she was short, highly coloured and not conventionally handsome. But she had ingrained dignity and a sense of bearing—and those who do not believe that such things are acquired with the blood royal would be obliged to give the credit for this to the training of the Duchess of Kent. When she first came to the throne and had held her first Levée and Drawing Room her uncle wrote to her: "Your *spirit* in all these new and trying proceedings makes me *happy beyond*

[61]There was generally in England a lowering of some of the barriers which had heretofore separated royal persons from ordinary mortals. Queen Victoria noticed in the late 1830's that her first cousin, Princess Augusta, daughter of George III's youngest son, the Duke of Cambridge, went out to balls and parties "like any other girl". Melbourne pointed out that this was the first time an English princess had ever done such a thing, and that he did not think that her grandfather George III, would have approved. He pointed out that the Princess ran the risk like other girls of forming attachments. And the Queen commented that this was "very true and very awkward". (*Girlhood*, vol. II, p. 150.)

[62]*Letters*, vol. I, p. 269.   [63]*Letters*, vol. II, p. 6.

expression."[64] A year later he wrote to say how sorry he had been to miss seeing her at a Review: "I feel always some regret at having been deprived of the happiness of seeing you *en fonc-tion* which you do in a degree of rare perfection."[65] The similar commendation from Lord Melbourne after her Coronation has often been quoted: "You did it beautifully—every part of it, with so much taste; it's a thing that you can't give a person advice upon: it must be left to a person."[66]

On this matter of the ceremonial side of the monarchy there is this point to be noted. Rather like the sleek and glossy coat which reflects the good condition of an animal, the British Court, based on an oligarchy of wealth and birth, reflected the well-being of the nation. A streak of arrogance may have been discernible, but the throng of people crowding into Bucking-ham Palace or St. James's Palace for an official function in the Queen's reign bore themselves bravely—moved with con-fidence and distinction. An American observer, who watched the Queen opening Parliament in 1857 has left this record of his impressions: "He [the American Minister] thinks it the most impressive sight he has yet witnessed, as the eye takes in at a glance the Sovereign, the Foreign Ministers, the nobility, ministers of state, and the members of both Lords and Com-mons. The Queen on this occasion looked even pretty. She wore a crown flashing with diamonds and a robe of cloth of gold. She delivered her address with effect, as she has a sweet voice, in addition to being a good reader, and rarely tremulous. She was agitated."[67] Certainly on all these formal occasions the Queen was greatly helped by the feeling that she was the head—

[64]*Letters*, vol. 1, p. 112. Of this Levée she wrote in her journal: "I had my hand kissed 3,000 times!"·

[65]*Letters*, vol. 1, p. 162.　　[66]*Letters*, vol. 1, p. 159

[67]This is from the *Journal of Benjamin Moran*, edited by Wallace and Gillespie, and published in 1948. The writer was secretary of the United States Legation in London, and he gives a fascinating picture of mid-Victorian life in England. Part of the value of what he writes lies in his lack of restraint. He does not hesitate to comment on occasions on the Queen's unbecomingly red face, and the crow's-feet which were already beginning to show round her eyes. He noted that she was evidently fond of dancing and music, and at a Court Ball he wrote: "I saw her once or twice singing the tune and shaking her head in the dance."

the outward and visible emblem—of all the pride and prosperity of the British peoples. As always the perceptive eye of King Leopold noticed this. In 1842 the Queen and Prince gave a crowded fancy-dress ball at Buckingham Palace at which the Prince appeared as King Edward III, and the Queen as Queen Philippe.[68] King Leopold wrote to his niece: "Your *fête* I believe to have been most probably one of the most splendid *ever* given. There is hardly a country where so much magnificence exists; Austria has some of the means, but the Court is not elegant from its nature."[69]

Although the Queen was given confidence by the magnificence of those who provided the background for her official entertaining, her own gifts and bearing were only enchanced by their splendour. The story has often been told how she captured the hearts of the Parisians on a state visit to the Paris opera when she advanced to the front of the box with complete confidence to bow to the audience while the Empress moved with uncertainty. The whole house rose and cheered while the cry *vive* was repeated so that the orchestra could not start playing "God save the Queen". And although this belongs to a later period of her life it illustrates the point. When her second son married the Czar's daughter in 1874, the Queen, though she had lived in retirement for thirteen years, broke her seclusion to appear at some of the celebrations. The Ladies of the Diplomatic Corps, who had hardly seen her, were immensely struck by the extremely graceful way—not assisted by her personal appearance or her clothes—in which she walked and moved and did her various civilities.[70] We can almost understand the ingenuous pride with which she once remarked that when she drove through Hyde Park the people always came running to greet her—a civility which they never showed "to Bertie and Alix".[71]

[68]It was of this function that the Queen wrote: "There is such asking, and so many silks and drawings and crowns, and God knows what, to look at, that I who hate being troubled about dress am quite *confuse.*" *Letters,* vol. 1, p. 493.

[69]The Emperor was at this time an imbecile. *Letters,* vol. 1, p. 497.

[70]*Notebooks of A Spinster Lady,* 1919.

[71]The Prince and Princess of Wales.

So under the influence of the Queen's happy and ordered domestic background her life began to assume a pattern of regularity. The beginning of the year was spent at Buckingham Palace and Windsor Castle with some formal entertaining and functions. The spring and the early summer were passed at Osborne, and then came Buckingham Palace for the summer and the height of the Victorian season. August saw the migration to Balmoral, and on coming south the Queen invariably spent some weeks of the early winter at Osborne. Christmas was spent at Windsor. Such was the cycle of her life—agreeable, varied—a life spent in high places but without luxury or extravagance and bounded by hard work.

And there remains the final change which marriage effected in her life. The Prince showed her that it was her duty to watch over the business of the nation, to restrain and if the need arose to goad the Government. Under Melbourne she had glided comfortably along the stream of affairs leaving the helm to him. In the early days of her marriage the Queen did not discuss public affairs with her husband. She regarded them as a matter between her and her ministers, and she confessed that she kept these things from the Prince largely through laziness because she preferred to talk to him on other topics.[72] The

[72] Political topics are not always an easy subject for discussion among friends and relations. The idea that related heads of states could solve all kinds of political difficulties by meeting and talking is not based on reality. Such exchanges could, as the Queen always sensed, lead to embarrassment. As a girl of nineteen she wrote to the King of the Belgians: "You must not, dear Uncle, think that it is from want of interest that I, in general, abstain from touching upon these matters [i.e. politics] in my letters to you: but I am fearful, if I were to do so, to change our present delightful and familiar correspondence into a formal and stiff discussion upon political matters, which would not be agreeable to either of us. . . ." Of course when it was necessary the Queen could and did write to a fellow sovereign expressing her country's point of view on a matter in dispute, but this was a different matter from introducing political matters into a family correspondence. (*Letters*, vol. 1, p. 173.) In the same way the Queen found it infinitely more agreeable to talk to the Prince on trifles than to discuss state business. She told Melbourne that she did not discuss such things with the Prince for fear that they might lead to difference of opinion. (*Letters*, vol. 1, p. 283.)

Prince, however, saw that this was not the whole reason, and that part of the explanation was that she did not really understand much of the business laid before her, and that it was therefore difficult for her to discuss such things and argue about them. He said that her absolute confidence in Melbourne and the Whigs made her "inattentive to the plans and measures proposed" and that she thought it unnecessary "entirely to comprehend them".[73]

At first after the fall of Melbourne she did attempt some independent comments on state affairs—but these were largely directed to preserving the principles which had governed Melbourne and the Whigs. She objected, for example, to the appointment of an Irish judge whom she believed to be an extreme Orangeman on the grounds that it might imperil the favourable effect produced in Ireland by the moderation of Whig rule.[74] She also pulled up Sir Robert Peel's government sharply, if she noted any neglect of the Queen's authority over appointments. A few weeks after the formation of his government she wrote to say that she had read in the papers that the British Ambassador to St. Petersburg had left to take up his appointment. She added: "The Queen can hardly believe this, as no Ambassador or Minister *ever* left England without previously asking for an Audience and receiving one, as the Queen always wishes to see them before they repair to their posts."[75]

And it was from now onwards that the Queen's comments—admonitory and sometimes querulous—were passed to ministers over the range of national life seen from the eminence of the throne. Perhaps rather like a headmistress the Queen expressed her views with the knowledge that they would spread but without the intention of laying down a rule. As whispers come from dormitories and cautionary undertones from girls on a country walk—"*She* does not really like us doing that"—

[73] *Letters*, vol. 1, p. 283.

[74] One of the chief successes of Melbourne lay in his handling of Ireland – largely explained by his refusal to use the extremists. There was sense and force therefore in this comment of the Queen. See the Queen's letter to Peel of 26 October 1841.

[75] *Letters*, vol. 1, p. 442.

so the prejudices and opinions of Queen Victoria became known and respected. When certain members of the House of Commons made difficulties on an obscure point affecting Ministers of the Scottish Church she expressed a hope to her Prime Minister that "every attempt will be made to put an end to what is really indecent conduct".[76] When the Court of Directors of the East India Company decided to recall a successful Governor-General, she told the Prime Minister that she thought it *very* unwise and very ungrateful and that she would not be sorry if "these gentlemen knew that that is her opinion".[77] When Sir Robert Peel, as Prime Minister, was in difficulty with some of his cabinet she expressed the hope that "none of his colleagues will prevent him from doing what it is *right* to do".[78] When a new Prime Minister was undertaking to form a government she told him that it was important that he should not recommend *Puseyites* and *Romanisers* for Church promotion.[79] When the Crimean War had started she wrote to one of the Cabinet: "The Queen seizes this opportunity of expressing her sense of the *imperative importance* of the Cabinet being united." She added that they should not let differences appear and that "the knowledge that they existed was a cause of GREAT *anxiety* to the Queen".[80]

Moreover the Queen through the officials at Court and through her private friends, had considerable knowledge about the characters and capabilities of people suggested to her to fill diplomatic, senior, and official positions. In some cases she was better equipped for commenting on such appointments than were her advisers. This was especially true of positions abroad because of her relationship and private correspondence with other royal persons. She kept up a weekly exchange of letters— fascinating because of their frankness—with her uncle in Brussels. Through him she was in touch with the reigning family of France from her accession till 1848. (The Queen of the Belgians was daughter to the King of the French.) She was also in regular correspondence with the Portuguese Royal Family—her first cousin had married the Queen—and from

[76]*Ibid.*, vol. I, p. 611.   [77]*Ibid.*, vol. II, p. 10.   [78]*Ibid.*, vol. II, p. 55.   [79]*Ibid.*, vol. II, p. 456.   [80]*Letters*, vol. III, p. 19.

the end of the 1840's with the heir to the Prussian throne and his wife. The Prince was closely informed on all German topics by his brother, the reigning Duke of Saxe-Coburg, and by Archduke John of Austria, the accomplished younger son of the Emperor Leopold II, who was his personal friend. Very early in the 1840's the Queen was objecting to the British Minister at the Hague,[81] who had indulged in some unwise pleasantries at the expense of King Leopold. The Queen began by the complaint that his abilities were "not of the first order" and then pressed for his removal "without being told that it was for his conduct".[82] And naturally on royal or dynastic questions the Queen had great advantages over her rather insular cabinets. Correcting a Foreign Office despatch, she pointed out that it was quite wrong to say that: "the Duke of Augustenbourg has *no* claim to the Danish Crown, his mother was the daughter of Christian VII and Queen Matilda."[83]

A more interesting situation arose when the Queen and Prince moved away from personalities into the world of politics. The picture of Europe drawn for them by their friends and relations was totally different from that prevailing in the Foreign Office, where Englishmen—largely insular and untravelled—peered into the strange land of Europe with wonder not dissimilar from that felt by Gulliver when he was dropped into the bowl of cream at the Court of Brobdingnag. The policy of successive British Governments at that time—that is to say in the two decades following the Queen's marriage—was to encourage all manifestations of Liberal feeling on the Continent, to make things difficult for the established Governments and to hold up Kings and Emperors to ridicule. Those who saw rather

[81]Sir Edward Disbrowe. Not for nothing did he carry the second name of Cromwell.

[82]*Letters*, vol. i, pp. 512, 523.

[83]*Ibid.*, vol. ii, p. 387. The Queen, though a little aloof from European royalties, was always meticulous on questions of precedence and who was who. She enjoyed thumbing through the Almanach de Gotha, and contemplating brides and bridegrooms for her children. When a foreign prince was suggested as a possible husband for one of her daughters she at once snubbed the suggestion because the young man could not dance the Fackel Tanz – a dance with torches confined to princes of the choicest blood.

more deeply, realised that the Kings were not quite so silly nor their bourgeois critics quite so virtuous as they appeared from the seclusion of Whitehall. The policy is generally and rightly associated with the blunt, splendid and patriotic personality of Palmerston, who had a John Bullish contempt for the Governments of Europe and felt that they would all really benefit from English advice and English example.[84] In his despatches to British Ambassadors Palmerston wrote very much as he spoke: he saw no reason for cloaking his feelings even though he knew that the Queen and the Prince would have to read what he had written before it was sent. One example (of many) shows the kind of thing which happened. The Queen objected to British policy in Portugal and the tone of the Foreign Office despatches: she sent a protest to the Prime Minister indignantly pointing out that the Portuguese sovereigns were "her near and dear relations".[85] In his reply Palmerston laid about him with gusto, pointing out that the Portuguese Royal Family were: "guided, I might almost say governed, by a pedantic and bigotted tutor, by a furious Portuguese Fanatic, by a newspaper editor, a vulgar man suddenly raised to power and full of low resentments, and by a gambling, drinking, unscrupulous Priest".[86] This was not exactly a flattering picture of the domestic bliss of the "near and dear relations".

There was in fact a cleavage, deep and complete, between the Court and the Foreign Office under Palmerston. It would be an over-simplification to say that the Queen and Prince were supporters of the dynasties—the Habsburgs in Vienna, Hohenzollerns in Berlin, Bourbon-Orleans in Paris and Braganza in Lisbon—while Palmerston supported the peoples in revolt against these masters. The truth was that the British Court favoured caution: they would have liked this country to support neither side. Palmerston would have argued that neutrality was out of the question: the plants, precariously sprouting, of Liberalism and parliamentary democracy needed the protection

[84] The most successful book on Palmerston because it is painted on a broad canvas is Kingsley Martin, *The Triumph of Lord Palmerston*, 1924.
[85] *Letters*, vol. II, p. 141.
[86] Quoted from Royal Archives in R. Fulford, *The Prince Consort*.

of Great Britain if they were ever to take root in the unfriendly soil of Europe. The Queen and Prince felt—not unreasonably—that their experiences of affairs and (in the Prince's
case) first-hand knowledge justified their making a contribution.

Palmerston became Foreign Secretary in the summer of 1846,
and for the next twenty years he dominated public life both
as Foreign Secretary and Prime Minister. He lent his name to
an epoch. But the party system during those twenty years was
confused: the Conservatives had foundered on Protection, while
the historic Whig Party was breaking up into Liberals and
Radicals. In consequence no Government was assured of a very
stable majority and an independent minister like Palmerston
was unrestrained by the pressure of a party following—at once
strong and united. The point is important, for the weakness
of Parliament gave the Crown its chance. In fact did not the
virtual absence of Parliamentary control explain and partially
excuse intervention by the Crown?

To survey the struggle in all its details is beyond the scope
of this book.[87] In a felicitous phrase Palmerston once said "events
are moving at a hand gallop". And they carried the dispute
between Palmerston and the Court from Portugal to France,
from France to Germany, from Germany to Hungary and on
to Italy, with Austria always as the bastion of reaction.
Although through the later 1840's the Queen and Prince
seriously canvassed the possibility of dismissing Palmerston, they
finally contented themselves with establishing the principle that
foreign office despatches should be submitted to them before
being sent, and that they were not to be altered after approval
by the Queen. In a memorandum to the Prime Minister in
August 1850 the Queen stated that if these principles were
broken she would consider the minister "as failing in sincerity
towards the Crown" and guilty of conduct which was a justi-
fication of "her constitutional right of dismissing the minister".[88]

[87]The reader is here referred to the published letters of the Queen. Where
these are thought too partial they can be corrected by Mr. Kingsley Martin's
book.

[88]*Letters*, vol. II, p. 315.

But only a twelvemonth later the quarrel blazed up once again. The Hungarian patriot Kossuth, who had once branded the Habsburgs as "perjured in the sight of God and man" and seemed the epitome of the revolutionary spirit of 1848, came to England in the autumn of 1851. He landed at Southampton, and moving up to London made a number of able but inflammatory speeches calling for a crusade against the Emperors of Russia and Austria. The Queen, as soon as Kossuth landed, wrote to the Prime Minister (Lord John Russell) asking him to prevent Lord Palmerston from receiving the Hungarian. After Kossuth's attacks on the Emperors, Lord John indicating that he spoke with the authority of the Queen wrote to his Foreign Secretary ending: "I must therefore positively request that you will not receive Kossuth." Palmerston flew into a rage and replied instanter while the Prime Minister's messenger waited: "I do not choose to be dictated to as to who I may or may not receive in my own house. . . . I shall use my own discretion . . . you will of course use yours as to the composition of your Government." The Queen then sent a letter to Palmerston, through the Prime Minister, demanding in her name that the reception of Kossuth should not take place. Lord John showed great patience, decided not to send the Queen's letter but laid the matter before the cabinet. Its members sided entirely with him, and Palmerston was thwarted. He revenged himself by receiving some loud-mouthed addresses from the Radicals of London in which the Emperors were dubbed "odious and detestable assassins". After this the Queen made it clear that she only endured Palmerston because his dismissal must lead to the break-up of Russell's following in the House of Commons. She wrote to Russell asking that he would explain to the cabinet that she only tolerated Palmerston as the lesser of two formidable ills. She insisted on their relations being brought before the cabinet, and although no resolution was adopted, regret was expressed at Palmerston's want of caution.[89]

But events moving out of control of a hand gallop and

[89]*Letters*, vol. II, p. 392ff. Spencer Walpole, *Life of Lord John Russell*, vol. II, p. 133.

assuming the wild manoeuvres of Gilpin's horse carried the
Queen and her Foreign Secretary to a still graver quarrel. The
British Ambassador in Paris at this time (Lord Normanby) was
brother to one of the Prince's private secretaries, and through
this family correspondence the Court realised that Palmerston
was bullying Normanby because he was thought antagonistic to
Louis Napoleon, who had on 2 December succeeded in a *coup
d'état* against the Republic. In a letter dated 9 December,
which was shown to the Queen, Lady Normanby told her
brother-in-law that Palmerston in conversation with the French
Ambassador in London expressed his entire approval of the
coup d'état. Taking advantage of this inside information the
Queen complained to Lord John: it became only too clear that
letters and despatches were being sent to Normanby which had
never been seen by either the Queen or the Prime Minister.
Goaded to decisive action the Prime Minister faced his Foreign
Secretary with his offence. On 22 December Palmerston was out.
On the next day the Queen wrote, with glee, to her uncle:
"I have the greatest pleasure in announcing to you a piece of
news which I know will give you as much satisfaction and
relief as it does to us, and will do to the *whole* of the world.
Lord Palmerston is no longer Foreign Secretary...."[90]

Nothing illustrates more clearly than her dealings with
Palmerston the absence of vindictiveness in the Queen's character. She was certainly capable of exulting when she got her
own way, but she did not bear malice. Only three and a half
years after she had written the words with which the pre-
ceding paragraph ends, she was writing to her uncle (6 February
1855) "Six o'clock p.m. One word to say that *Lord Palmerston*

[90]*Ibid.*, vol. II, p. 417. In old age Russell regretted that he had not seen
Palmerston, reminded him of the conditions to which he had agreed
and insisted on his respecting them. Moreover Lord Normanby was somewhat woolly in his advice to the Foreign Office, for, as Guizot once said:
"Il est bon enfant, mais il ne comprend pas notre langue." The Norman-
bys were practised courtiers—Lady Normanby had been one of the
Queen's Ladies of the Bedchamber—and understood the art of whispering
welcome tidings where they would be heard by royalty. As the Queen herself
was fond of observing—it is hard for royal persons to learn the truth.

has just *kissed* hands as *Prime* Minister."[91] And a year later she was writing to offer him the Garter as a public token of her approval of "his zealous and able" conduct of affairs.[92]

There is one side issue on this question of the Queen's relations with politicians which deserves notice. Liberals or progressive politicians are generally more considerate to royal persons than are Conservatives. The trouble taken by Lord John Russell to meet the Queen's wishes over Palmerston contrasts rather strangely with the behaviour of a Conservative Prime Minister, Lord Derby, in not dissimilar circumstances. After the Indian Mutiny and the assumption of control of India by the Government from the East India Company, Lord Derby's son, then Lord Stanley, was the Secretary for India. He had been one of the brilliant circle at Cambridge known as "The Apostles" but he was a difficult and wayward politician. In February 1859 the Queen wrote to Derby warning him (so that he might not be taken by surprise) of a possible unseemly public difference between herself and his son, and complaining that every act of Stanley's had been "destructive of the power and influence of the Crown". Derby was an extremely wise man—far more astute than John Russell—and after stating that the letter had caused him "deep pain", he thought that he had no alternative but to resign, and that he must certainly submit the letter to his cabinet colleagues. The Queen, realising that she had gone too far, asked that the letter should be returned and that Lord Derby would consider it as not having been written.[93]

By the end of the 1840's the Queen and Prince had established Buckingham Palace as an adjunct of Government—a cautionary department not altogether unlike the Cabinet office of a later day. The inmates of the Palace watched with un-blinking vigilance the whole range of the Government, seeking information, proffering advice and occasionally spurring on-wards. The majority of the political correspondence of the 1840's and 1850's was the work of the Prince: the idiom makes it

[91]*Letters*, vol. III, p. 128. [92]*Ibid.*, vol. III, p. 237.
[93]*Letters*, vol. III, p. 404.

fairly easy to distinguish the Prince's work from that of the Queen's, though almost all the official letters were signed by the Queen and based on drafts prepared by the Prince. The following request for information is characteristic of the system in action:

10 January 1844

The Queen understands that there is a negotiation with Sweden and Denmark pending about the cessation of their tribute to Morocco, likewise that Prince Metternich has sent a despatch condemning as unfair the understanding come to between us and France about the Spanish Marriage: that there is a notion of exchanging Hong-Kong for a more healthy Colony.

The Queen, taking a deep interest in all these matters, and feeling it her duty to do so, begs Lord Aberdeen to keep her always informed of what is on the *tapis* in his Department.[94]

The reader would be mistaken in picturing the Queen and Prince as mere advisers to the cabinet—showering their ministers with what the great newspaper editor (Delane) once called "that most cruel of all inflictions—good advice". The Queen was—both in small ways and large—of great service to the Government. Her suggestions on trifling matters were not always followed: she thought that the abbreviation V.C. was a mistake: abbreviations in general use like M.P. for Member of Parliament or K.G. for Knight of the Garter designated a person: "no one can be called a Victoria Cross": she therefore urged the abbreviation B.V.C.—Bearer of the Victoria Cross.[95] On the other hand many of her suggestions were followed—for example the adoption of the name British Columbia instead of New Caledonia for the Colony on the west coast of Canada.[96] And even on the greatest issues, in that monarchical age, the Queen was a great help to the Government. One example of this was her correspondence with the Emperor of Russia just before the Crimean War. Certainly she consulted both the Prime Minister and Foreign Secretary but parts of the

[94]*Ibid.*, vol. II, p. 4.   [95]*Ibid.*, vol. III, p. 298.   [96]*Letters*, vol. III, p. 376.

letters were entirely her own. The Foreign Secretary told the diarist Greville that she wrote an answer in French, and that "it was a very good one".[97] On another occasion she explained to the Foreign Secretary that she always wrote personally to the Emperor Napoleon to tell him any family event and that as she was writing to announce the birth of her grandson (the future Kaiser) she would include some political comments if the Government would provide her with "the heads of the matter" which they wished said to him.[98] Although the letters of the Queen to her fellow sovereigns were, according to precedent, polite and formal they were written with the same frankness which marked the correspondence of the Queen with her own ministers. To the Czar she said: *Mais quelle que soit la pureté des motifs qui dirigent les actions du Souverain même le plus élevé par le caractère. Votre Majesté sait que les qualités personnelles ne sont point suffisantes dans des transactions internationales par lesquelles un Etat se lie envers un autre en de solennels engagements...*" To the Emperor's brother-in-law, the King of Prussia, who was following a policy of craven neutrality at the beginning of the Crimean War she wrote: "I have hitherto looked upon Prussia as one of the Great powers which, since the peace of 1815, have been guarantors of treaties, guardians of civilisation, defenders of the right, and real arbiters of the Nations, and for my part I have felt the divine responsibility of this sacred office, without undervaluing at the same time the heavy obligation, not unconnected with danger, which it imposes on me. If you, dear Sir and Brother, abdicate these obligations, you have also abdicated that position for Prussia." And she went on to say that what she had written "flows from the affectionate heart of a sister, who could not pardon herself, were she not, at so weighty a moment, to let you see into her inmost soul".

There was great advantage in these forthright communications because a foreign government could not pretend that

---

[97]Greville, vol. VI, p. 463.

[98]*Letters,* vol. III, p. 402. The draft of the letter will be found in *Letters,* vol. III, pp. 402–3 and the version as sent on p. 367 of vol. IV, of Theodore Martin's *Life of the Prince Consort.*

they were ignorant of British feelings and intentions. If there
is truth in the assertion that in 1914 Germany was in the dark
about British policy then it is much to be regretted that Queen
Victoria's grandson (King George V) did not sit down and
write to his first cousin in Berlin with the trenchant clarity
of his grandmother.[99]

Helped by the presence of monarchies throughout Europe,
but largely through their own industry and capabilities, the
Queen and Prince revolutionised the idea of monarchy. Influence was substituted for power: respectability and hard work
took the place of picturesque indulgence. "To-morrow is the
eighteenth anniversary of my blessed marriage, which has
brought such universal blessings on this country and Europe!
For *what* has not my beloved and perfect Albert done? Raised
monarchy to the *highest* pinnacle of *respect*, and rendered it
popular *beyond* what it *ever* was in this country."[100] Her own
services in this respect she ignores. Yet they were of course
considerable. But the question now looms ominously on the
horizon how would she prosper when "the beloved and perfect
one" was withdrawn? How would she fare alone?

III

That the queen would bend before the incalculable disaster
of the Prince's premature death was inevitable. Not only was
her devotion to him absolute but her reliance on him was complete. Her feelings for him and her misery at his departure
are too familiar to need the comments or analysis of someone
outside. All is obvious from her own writings. One point,
however, merits emphasis. Her children occupied a place far
below her husband in her affections, and therefore it was not
possible for them to fill the blank when he was gone. She has

[99] The Tsar and Emperor did exchange long telegrams in 1914 in something the style of the Queen: these did at one moment, as the Czar said,
give "a glimmer of hope". King George's silence was marked and, in its
consequences, unfortunate.

[100] *Letters*, vol. III, p. 335.

explained this very clearly, during the lifetime of the Prince, to her friend the Princess of Prussia.[101] Writing from Balmoral in 1856 she said: "I see the children much less and even here, where Albert is often away all day long, I feel no especial pleasure or compensation in the company of the elder children.... And only very occasionally do I find the rather intimate intercourse with them either agreeable or easy.... I only feel properly à mon aise and quite happy when Albert is with me."

His death therefore left the Queen in a peculiar solitude. And in addition to her feelings of despair she had absorbed the respect for death and the indulgence of sorrow which were the characteristics of her age and divide it most sharply from our own. Long before the Prince's death she wrote to her uncle with almost ghoulish relish after seeing Lady Peel (the Prime Minister's wife) for the first time after her husband's death— "*Hers* is indeed a *broken heart*: she is so *truly* crushed by the *agony* of *her* grief; it was *very* touching to see and to hear her. Poor thing! She *never* can be happy again."[102] Such sentiments were, it will be understood, the insignia of Victorian widowhood to be assumed with the veil, the crêpe and the bombazine. But beneath "the sad caps" (as her youngest daughter, Princess Beatrice, in childhood called the Queen's widow's veil) the personality of the Queen remained. With the fortitude and obstinacy of her Hanoverian ancestors she fought to beat down grief, and carry on the Prince's work: her realism saved her from becoming abject: her dislike of humbug saved her from false consolations. (When a divine wrote to condole and told her that "henceforth Christ himself will be your husband" she flashed out to a friend, "That is what I call twaddle."[103])

[101]She was a liberal-minded and enlightened woman, who was born a princess of Saxe-Weimar, the grand-daughter of Goethe's friend and patron. She married Prince William of Prussia, afterwards King, and first German Emperor. She was the life-long friend of Queen Victoria whose letters to her were edited and published by Mr. Hector Bolitho in 1938.

[102]*Letters,* vol. II, p. 335.

[103] G. K. A. Bell, *Life of Randall Davidson, Archbishop of Canterbury,* 1935.

The circumstances of the Prince's death do not reveal any dark shadows across the Queen's personality: they rather reveal the finer and stronger side of it. The Prince became ill at the end of November 1861—at a time when he was disturbed by some youthful escapades of the Prince of Wales,[104] by the grievous illness of his youngest son and by the death of the King of Portugal and two of his brothers from typhoid fever. At the beginning of December the Prince was handed over to the full discipline of Victorian doctors who pronounced that he was suffering from "low fever": this turned to typhoid, with congestion of the lungs, which caused his death shortly before 11 o'clock on the night of 14 December 1861.

From the very start of the illness—as her *Journal* shows—the Queen was anxious. She did not, however, reveal her full feelings either to her uncle in Brussels or to the Prince's brother at Coburg—largely through fear that her apprehension might reach back to the sick-room at Windsor.[105] Now it is here that many writers on the Queen leave the hard road of fact for the delights of fancy. They picture the Queen—self-centred, robust, full of vitality, and unable to imagine mortal illness in others or that other human beings did not share her own vigorous habit of life. From here such writers slide into the argument that she almost believed that her position shielded her from the common fatalities of mankind: they would reinforce their case by the amusing (but apocryphal) story that when the *Victoria and Albert* yacht struck a huge wave, she sent for the Captain and said, "That must not occur again." Having placed the Queen among the Gods as believing herself sacrosanct from the encroachments of mortality they then picture the reality descending on her with shattering force. The story is dramatic but false. No one could read the account of the Prince's death, based on information provided by the Queen, without realising that she was, in her own words, "so anxious, so distressed" from the

[104]See R. Fulford, *The Prince Consort*, p. 264.
[105]Brussels was a great sounding board of gossip. Only a few months previously – at the time of the death of the Duchess of Kent – the story was spread from there through Europe that grief had destroyed the Queen's reason.

first day of the illness.[106] But writers having gone so far in their
fairy tale naturally crown it by depicting the Queen as giving
way, with abandon, to the shock of finding her husband dead.
A favourite version is that her screams rang through the Castle
walls when she realised that she had lost him for ever. We should
certainly have to endow the Queen's voice with superhuman
qualities if we believe that it penetrated the walls of Windsor
Castle. Another version, much favoured, is that she fell sense-
less on the body and had to be dragged away.[107] The only people
in the room at the time were the Queen and members of the
family, the Dean of Windsor, the doctors, the Prince's valet
and three members of the Prince's staff. None of them was
likely to chatter about this peculiarly private occasion. Ten years
after the Prince's death the Queen wrote an account of what
had happened based from rough jottings she had made at the
time. (Her *Journal*, meticulously kept from her earliest years,
abruptly stops on the day before the Prince's death and was
not started again for several weeks.) In her account the Queen
explains that she was sitting by the bed and when she realised
that the Prince had died she kissed his forehead and then rose,
crying out an exclamation of endearment. She then dropped on
her knees, and was helped up and led from the room by her
nephew and one of the Prince's secretaries.[108] Some readers might
think that these private matters are best left interred in the
unfathomable past, but the accepted story is absolutely unjust to
the Queen and needs correction. The Prince's Private Secretary

[106]*Life of the Prince Consort*, vol. v, p. 428 to end.
[107]The two authorities for this are Augustus Hare's Autobiography and
the *Notebooks of a Spinster Lady*. Though entertaining books they are
freely sprinkled with gossip, and both writers are imagining what happened
from their knowledge of how Victorian widows were expected to behave.
Even one of the best-informed of Victorian gossips believed that the doctors
had forbidden the Queen to kiss the Prince for fear of infection; see
George Villiers, *A Vanished Victorian*, 1938.
[108]From information in the Royal Archives. I acknowledge with gratitude the gracious permission of Her Majesty The Queen to use this source.
I am likewise indebted to the Duke of Wellington for letting me see a
private letter from his relative, the then Dean of Windsor, which exactly
bears out Queen Victoria's account of what happened.

said that although the Queen was beaten to the ground by grief "her self-control and good sense were wonderful".[109]

Since mediaeval times the personal misfortunes of our sovereigns have only rarely brought the Government machine to a halt. King Henry VIII's divorce is one example: George III's sudden attack of madness in the autumn of 1788 is another, and the death of the Prince is a third. The Prince's illness and death were, in the words of the Prime Minister, "matters of momentous public importance". When news of his death reached Downing Street the Prime Minister burst into tears. The untimely death of a leader of the nation at the age of forty-two is sufficient to explain the feelings of consternation which paralysed Whitehall and the capital. The immediate question was how the Queen would face a resumption of the essential business of the country. One portent was encouraging. The Queen herself was determined to carry on her work. On the advice of her uncle she left Windsor so as not to be there while the funeral was taking place in St. George's Chapel. As the special train carried her from Windsor she was heard repeating to herself "I will, I *will* do my duty."[110] For several weeks she stayed in seclusion at Osborne able to sign urgent papers and to correspond with Cabinet Ministers through the Prince's private secretaries.[111]

She held her first council three weeks after the Prince's death. The Privy Councillors sat in the Prince's sitting room,

[109]Edgar Sheppard, *Life of the Duke of Cambridge*, 1906.

[110]George Villiers, *A Vanished Victorian*, 1938.

[111]At that time the Queen had no private secretary. The Prince, with his private secretaries, had arranged all official business for her. The Government had always been nervous of the Queen having a secretary in case he should come between them and the Sovereign. But after 1861 circumstances made it essential for her to have the advice and help of the Prince's staff, but she was always careful not to offend the susceptibilities of ministers by openly making use of an official who was not recognised. She apologised to Palmerston for writing to him through General Grey, one of the Prince's secretaries. The matter was not regularised till 1866, when Grey was recognised as her private secretary, and officially appointed. On his death Sir Henry Ponsonby was appointed in 1870, and Sir Arthur Bigge (afterwards Lord Stamfordham) was appointed on Sir Henry's death in 1895.

while the Queen remained in her own room with the communicating door open. The clerk of the Privy Council, who was with the Privy Councillors, spoke on behalf of the Queen the word "Approved".[112] But as a member of the Court noted— "She has continued to work, but it has been as work and without interest."[113]

Then by degrees she started to see the ministers, beginning with those, like Lord Granville, with whom she was on terms of private friendship. In March she saw Gladstone, who was Chancellor of the Exchequer. They discussed affairs for a quarter of an hour and then the Queen, lowering her head and struggling with emotion, said "the nation has been very good to me in my time of sorrow".[114]

The burden of work which faced the Queen was onerous. She wished to carry on the supervision of government business which she and the Prince had established. She had also to control the upbringing of her eight unmarried children, and to assume responsibility for the smooth running of the entire Court. All these things she had in reality left to the Prince. "Hitherto," she said, "the Prince has thought for me."[115]

Certainly the Queen's preoccupation with business drew her back from the abyss of despair. She was also comforted by some words which the Prince had written to her after the death of her mother, the Duchess of Kent—"Pain is felt chiefly by dwelling on it and can thereby be heightened to an unbearable extent."[116] She was also comforted by the thought that death, which would re-unite her to the Prince, could not be far off. Woe betide the person who had the temerity to say that she was well! To her uncle, who had been told that she seemed well, she wrote: "I have been very unwell the whole time ... when I talk I get excited and flushed and very feverish, and that THEY call being well."[117]

[112]A somewhat similar procedure was followed when King George V was in bed, in 1928, at the beginning of his serious illness.

[113]*Letters*, Second Series, vol. i, p. 19.

[114]Morley, *Life of Gladstone*, vol. ii, p. 89.

[115]Sidney Lee, *Queen Victoria*, 1904.

[116]R. Fulford, *Life of the Prince Consort.*

[117]*Letters*, Second Series, vol. i, p. 62.

But if her spirits remained subdued her spirit began to rise. Did she not herself say in one of the first letters she wrote after the Prince's death: "My spirit rises when I think any wish or plan of his is to be touched or changed, or I am to be *made* to do anything."[118] Fortified by bound volumes of her husband's correspondence and memoranda she bent herself to the task of keeping alive his influence, his point of view with successive Governments. "They are Gospel now," she sobbed as she consulted them with the devotion of a fundamentalist. On many occasions—as her published correspondence shows—she pressed the teaching from these sacred books on her Government. Her methods are illustrated by the tangled case of the Duchies of Schleswig-Holstein. These formed the rather narrow tongue of land which connected Germany with Denmark: they were strategically important because they had a long frontage to the North Sea on one side and to the Baltic on the other. They included Kiel. The population of Holstein was wholly German, that of Schleswig partly German: both principalities were coveted by Prussia. The Kings of Denmark were also Dukes of Schleswig-Holstein: the duchies and Denmark were therefore joined by personal rule only—not unlike Hanover and Great Britain in the eighteenth century. This fairly simple matter was confused by a dynastic imbroglio, the disentangling of which needed the patience of an antiquarian and the zest of a genealogist. The Salic Law, Christians, Fredericks and heavy princes of the mighty house of Schleswig-Holstein-Sonderbourg-Augustenbourg tease the reader; they justify the famous remark of Palmerston who once said, in despair, that only two people understood the question: one (the Prince Consort) was dead and the other was mad. It is sufficient to say that when the King of Denmark died in 1863 —and Queen Victoria was highly indignant that he should have done so[119]—the Danish throne passed to his nearest relative in the female line—King Christian IX, who was Queen Alex-

[118]*Ibid.*, vol. III, p. 106.

[119]"This death of the King of Denmark is a terrible business... We were on the point of getting matters on a *fair* train of settlement when this wretched King dies." *Letters*, Second Series, vol. I, p. 116.

andra's father. Succession through the female line was not recognised in the duchies, and another Prince (also Christian) stepped forward to claim them, although his father had been paid £350,000 to give up his rights ten years earlier. German opinion and Queen Victoria warmly espoused the claim of this second Prince Christian to the duchies. In 1864 Prussia, supported by Austria, seized the duchies. Perhaps resolute action by other European powers might have stopped Prussia—it was the last chance of checking a fatal career of lawlessness—but the Prime Minister (Palmerston) and the Foreign Secretary (Russell) were both old, and imbued with outmoded terrors of the French. At the time the Queen was pressing forward the German point of view—so vehemently that on 4 January 1864 Palmerston wrote: "Viscount Palmerston can quite understand your Majesty's reluctance to take any active part in measures in any conflict against Germany, but he is sure that your Majesty will never forget that you are Sovereign of Great Britain, and that the honour of your Majesty's crown and the interests of your Majesty's Dominions will always be the guide of your Majesty's conduct."[120] Few constitutional sovereigns can have had a clearer rebuke from their leading minister than this. The Queen, who was always quick to realise when she had gone too far, made private enquiries and contented herself with the explanation for this letter that Palmerston was "gouty". However, when Russell made the same point she rapped out to him: "She must observe that she does not require to be reminded of the honour of England, which touches her more nearly than anyone else."[121] And now unluckily the Queen's sympathies in the dispute began to be noised abroad, and Palmerston had to urge her to be cautious in what she and members of the Court said. In May 1864 she was trounced in the House of Lords by Lord Ellenborough, a former Governor-General of India, for influencing the Government in a pro-German direction in the manner of the earlier Hanoverians. The Queen's indignation knew no bounds and she wrote to Russell, who had defended

[120]*Letters*, Second Series, vol. 1, p. 140.
[121]*Ibid.*,

her: "The Queen hopes everyone *will* know *how* she resents Lord Ellenborough's conduct and how she despises him."[122]

Such battles roused her; they prevented her from falling into a torpor of grief. They likewise illustrate the peculiar difficulties in which she was placed by the dynastic loyalties of her immediate family circle. Her eldest daughter (the Crown Princess of Prussia), though critical of some aspects of Prussian policy, warmly espoused the independence of the duchies from Denmark under "Fritz Augustenbourg."[123] The Queen's half sister, whose daughter had married Fritz Augustenbourg, was also a warm supporter of the independence of the duchies. The Prince and Princess of Wales were naturally vociferous in support of Danish claims to the duchies. In the winter of 1863 these princes and princesses all met at Windsor and the ruffling of plumage, cackling and pecking must have been intolerable. According to the Queen these royal battles became "very violent": and she felt mortified that there was no one "to *put* the *others* down" and to support her authority. Wisely her uncle wrote: "I deplore it for you. You must forbid it in your rooms."[124] While humbler families quarrel over wills or the disposition of a great-aunt's furniture, the calm of royal houses can be disturbed by political squabbles, which, as they are of larger consequence, cause a deeper storm. We can sympathise with Queen Victoria in these matters: she felt them as a grievous addition to her burdens. "My work and my worries," she wrote, "are so totally different to anyone else's."[125] But the interest of Schleswig-Holstein lies in the fact that it was the last of the attempts of the Crown, skilfully conducted while the Prince lived, to divert government policy by displaying a mastery of the facts and an understanding of the problem superior to those of the cabinet. This involved the Queen in a serious dispute with "those two dreadful old men", as she

[122]*Ibid.*, Second Series, vol. 1, p. 198.

[123]He was the eldest son of the Augustenbourg branch of the Schleswig-Holstein family: it was his father, Prince Christian, who had agreed to abandon his rights to the duchies in return for £350,000.

[124]*Letters*, Second Series, vol. 1, pp. 117, 124.

[125]*Ibid.*, p. 65.

called Russell and Palmerston, and the real danger of a public
attack on the Crown. The Queen learned from it—if not consciously then by instinct—that single-handed she could not
continue to guide the policy of her ministers.

And in this connexion her isolation and seclusion are important. She must have realised that she was far less well placed
to interfere on public issues than in the old days when she and
the Prince were in the middle of the broad stream of English
life—meeting all sections of the nation in a way that was not
even possible for a Prime Minister. Political interference was
not compatible with isolation. But looking back we can see
how impossible it was for the Queen, in widowhood, to go
back to the monarchical splendour of the 1840's and 1850's.
For we can see—perhaps more clearly than our ancestors could
—that there was something incongruous about all the paraphernalia of a court—the ceremonial, the trumpets and the
obeisance to introduce what she herself called "the spectacle of
a poor, broken-hearted widow, nervous and shrinking, ALONE
in STATE as a *show*". At the same time we can see how the
public, accustomed above all in Victorian times to value for
any expenditure of money, felt that they were getting scant
return for what they contributed to the upkeep of the monarchy.
In the forty years of her widowhood the Queen perhaps slept
twenty nights at Buckingham Palace, so that we can understand
the Victorian wag who posted up on the railings of Buckingham Palace a placard which read: "This desirable residence
to let—the owner having declined business."

The difference between what the public expected and the
reality is illustrated by an anecdote about the Vice-Master of
Trinity College, Cambridge, Adam Sedgwick, who was an old
friend of the Prince Consort's. He went to visit the Queen, in
widowhood, and when he got back to Cambridge one of those
fashionable chirrupers, who abound in university life, greeted
him by saying: "Oh Vice-Master, I hear you've been to
Court." "No, madam," he replied, "I have *not* been to
Court: I have been to see a Christian woman in her affliction."[126]

[126]*Life and Letters of Adam Sedgwick*, 1890, vol. II, p. 382.

Four years after the Prince's death she made a great effort and opened Parliament in person. For the first time she drove through the London streets with a military escort and with some ceremony. She has described her feelings: "It was a fearful moment for me when I entered the carriage *alone,* and the band played: also when all the crowds cheered, and I had great difficulty in repressing my tears."[127]

For some months before this opening of Parliament by the Queen, which was in February 1865, *The Times* had been agitating for her to take a more public part in the nation's life. The paper had particularly urged that visiting foreign notabilities should be entertained by the Queen and that, if she could not appear herself, she might offer them accommodation in Buckingham Palace. As the paper said, London hotels were so bad that they had become nothing more than a refuge for the homeless. After a particularly outspoken article in 1864 the Queen took the extraordinary step of writing a letter to *The Times* in her own hand. This was published not in the correspondence columns but prominently, under the heading "The Court". The point of this communication was that the Queen had to discharge "other and higher duties" than those of "mere representation". It was these duties which weighed on her, "overwhelming her with work and anxiety"; they prevented her from undertaking the fatigue of state ceremonies. She denied explicitly that she was about to resume her old place in society.[128]

Delane, who was then editor of *The Times*, shrewdly put his finger on the weak place in the Queen's contention: "They who would isolate themselves from the world ... must be content to let things take their course."[129] While he perhaps exaggerated in saying that the Queen lived in the shadows of a bygone time, he was perfectly correct in hinting that by im-

[127]*Letters,* Second Series, vol. 1, p. 298.

[128]For the forty years of her widowhood the Queen never went to a theatre or a concert. She held drawing-rooms and levees, but she does not appear to have given or attended a court ball.

[129]*The Times,* 1 April 1864.

muring herself from the world she was unfitting herself for those "other and higher duties" at which she toiled away. On the great issues of the 1860's—the extension of the franchise, the provision of improved education, the Irish Church or the volunteers, what real contribution could be made by the hermit, dwelling in the Isle of Wight, the Thames Valley or the Highlands of Scotland and speeding between them in the privacy of a special train? The contrast is obvious and glaring when the reader compares the royal memoranda of the Prince's time with those sent by the Queen thereafter. The former—critical, balanced and informed—might have come from any minister in response to a cabinet paper circulated to members of the Government: after the Prince's death the royal memoranda are certainly not useless: but they become more in the nature of diatribes. Even with the help of her able secretariat she could not hope to make valuable comments on details of legislation. As Delane pointed out, people "living in the shadows of a bygone time" are apt to give way to feelings upon the questions of the day. Delane was of course perfectly right. The danger was that a woman, living in seclusion like some Chinese potentate, might force her feelings, prejudices and even presentiments on the cabinet. Although the Queen had her full share of these, and frequently paraded them before her ministers, part of her genius lay in knowing how far she could legitimately press them. In fact she developed into a kind of referee—sometimes capricious and tiresome—but on the whole prudent and reasonable. Abandoning the task of detailed criticism, she became rather the vigilant custodian of what she thought was public opinion. All framers of policy realised that their measures would have to be subjected to this severe scrutiny. The development of this role by the Queen lends importance to her middle years as she begins to emerge from the deepest shadows of her grief.

She was of course always accustomed to her own way: an expression of her wishes was sufficient: if they caused heartburnings in other people that was of no consequence. The well-being of the monarchy, and the smooth running of her life were the consideration against which all others perished. We see this particularly clearly in her dealings with her family.

Hardly a year after the Prince's death, the Greek people, whom the Queen described as "very fanciful and touchy", offered their throne to her second son Prince Alfred, "our darling boy, so like his beloved father, so clever and talented and so excessively amiable".[130] In spite of this eulogy he developed into one of the most unpopular and disagreeable of English Princes: but the Greeks, unconscious of what the fates had in store for the Prince, voted overwhelmingly for him as their king in a plebiscite of the nation. He received in fact 23,000 votes with the nation's second choice receiving only 2,400. Garibaldi received 3 votes, and four French candidates were bottom of the poll with a single vote. But a stronger force than the wayward electors of Greece made itself heard: "Upon no earthly account and under no circumstances would she ever assent to it,"[131] she told a member of the Government. In the result the throne passed to a brother of Queen Alexandra who had received six votes in the plebiscite.

In the management of her family, we notice that she had a natural inclination to put people to right. No one could be in doubt what the Queen thought, for she loved to give all and sundry her decisive, clear-cut opinions. When the Prince of Wales's eldest son was born she wrote to the Prince stating what the child was to be called and naming the god-parents to be invited in addition to "your own old Mama" (she was forty-five). She took advantage of this opportunity to tell the Prince that when he succeeded to the throne he would be known as King Albert Edward, and she added that it would be "impossible" and "monstrous" for him to drop the Albert.[132] Her capacity for laying down the law—especially on all aspects of marriages—was by no means confined to her own children and descendants. She wrote to her uncle in 1863 that she had taken advantage of his younger son's birthday to write to him "*in very strong terms*" about his marrying. And she added rather

[130]*Letters*, Second Series, vol. 1, p. 68.

[131]*Letters*, p. 48.

[132]When the time came he dropped Albert, and King George VI likewise shied away from the name when he came to the throne in 1937. Queen Victoria would have thought each decision deserving her severest strictures. (*Letters*, Second Series, vol. 1, p. 152.)

ominously: "I love him dearly, but I own I do not think him improved in *essential* qualities."[133] When one of the favourite members of the Court—Lady Augusta Bruce, who was Woman of the Bedchamber and permanently with the Queen— became engaged to Dean Stanley, her marriage was announced to King Leopold by Queen Victoria in the following terms: "You will be sorry to hear that my dear Lady Augusta ... at 41, without a previous long attachment, has, most unnecessarily decided to *marry* ! ! ... *I* thought she *never* would leave *me*."[134]

We have seen in these dealings with her family how she expected people to accept what she said as final—even on matters (like the upbringing of their own children) which were really their own concern. In the same way the members of the Court could not hope to avoid snubs and rebukes. Yet the Queen's methods had this advantage; they showed people exactly where they stood with the Queen, and that she was not speaking them fair but grumbling behind their backs. In 1866 a vacancy in one of the highest positions at Court occurred: she wrote to Lord Charles Fitzroy[135] explaining perfectly frankly that she was going to pass him over and entering "confidentially into the reasons which have influenced her choice".[136]

The extent to which she was uninfluenced by what people thought or said is illustrated by the case of John Brown. The introduction of this Highland ghillie into the inner circle of Court life, after the Prince's death, was too much for the decorum of even the Victorians. In the familiar painting by Landseer of the Queen on a pony, whose head is held by Brown, the prevailing colour of the picture is black, and wits repeated, as they gazed at the representation of their sovereign, "All is black that is not brown." In 1866 *Punch* published a mock court-circular, which ran thus:

[133]*Letters*, Second Series, vol. 1, p. 82. This was the father of King Albert of the Belgians.
[134]*Ibid.*, p. 114.
[135]Afterwards 7th Duke of Grafton, who died in 1918, aged ninety-five.
[136]*Letters*, Second Series, vol. 1, p. 302.

Balmoral, *Tuesday*

Mr. John Brown walked on the slopes.

He subsequently partook of a haggis

In the evening *Mr. John Brown* was pleased to listen to a
bag-pipe

Mr. John Brown retired early.[137]

Naturally enough posterity, searching for romance in the most
improbable places, has vulgarly magnified a perfectly simple
relationship into love and marriage. The Queen has herself explained both in her *Journal* and in a letter to her uncle that she
made Brown her confidential servant because of his particular
gifts of insight and understanding.[138] In other words he could
arrange matters to her liking without constantly bothering her
with questions. But this elevation of the Scotsman naturally
caused jealousies and annoyed the Queen's children. Mr. Ivor
Brown happily expresses the truth when he likens Brown to
"a lonely Scottish fir" amid the gentler plantations at Windsor
and to "an abiding thistle" on the trim lawns of Buckingham
Palace.[139]

The matter seems only once to have come into the open and,
like all strong characters, the Queen showed that she knew
exactly when she had to give way. In the summer of 1867 she
proposed that Brown should attend her at an important review
in Hyde Park. (This was subsequently cancelled because of the
execution of the Emperor Maximilian of Mexico.) The annoyance caused among the confidential circle of the Queen by
Brown being present on this occasion was deep. The principal
objectors were almost certainly the Prince of Wales and the
Commander-in-Chief, that stalwart traditionalist the Duke of
Cambridge,[140] and it will be remembered that the public gossip

[137]E. E. P. Tisdall, *Queen Victoria's John Brown*, 1938.

[138]It was officially stated in the Court Circular, when Brown died in
1883, that he never once absented himself from duty for a single day,
though it is believed that he was occasionally incapacitated by a fancy for
the whisky bottle.

[139]Ivor Brown, *Balmoral*, 1955.

[140]Queen Victoria had always been somewhat out of sympathy with this
first cousin since he had been brought forward as a possible bridegroom

about Brown was at this time at its height. The Queen wrote to one of her equerries that she was astonished and shocked at an attempt being made by some people to prevent her faithful servant going with her to the Review. "What it all means she does *not* know." She asked that her equerries should set the matter right for the future, "*whatever* may be done on this single occasion."[141] It would appear that after this the Queen was more careful in employing Brown on state occasions as distinct from private ones. But in general her attachment to the Highlander shows how she was capable of continuing on her course, superbly indifferent to the clamour of the public or the pressure of her family.

As the years go on and she begins to emerge from what she calls—with pathetic understatement—"my misfortune" her strength as a public character grows clearer. She would perhaps have argued that she was able to assume authority over her family, over the Court and to an extent over the government because as her life was ended (a phrase to which she was especially attached) she could look on affairs with the impartiality of one who—if not in tune with the infinite—was largely withdrawn from temporal affairs. She could for example write to a cabinet minister: "The things of this world are of no interest to the Queen: her thoughts are *fixed above*".[142] To this idea she would have clung as the explanation for her personal sway. But yet we, coming afterwards and reading her letters and journals, can see that whatever she may have fancied, the picture which she thus drew of herself was powerful but imaginative. "You cling to life," the Prince Consort had once told her. This was the truth. Even in the depths of misery when she assured her uncle that she was not likely to live so long as people supposed, she hastily added that for the sake of the children, "I feel a *few* more years would be desirable."[143] And

in early days. He became very friendly with the Prince of Wales partly owing to his relationship with the Princess.

[141]*Letters*, Second Series, vol. 1, pp. 433-4.
[142]*Ibid.*, p. 9.
[143]*Ibid.*, p. 92.

when her carriage was upset in the Highlands, through the antics of a tipsy coachman, she wondered whether they were all about to be killed, but quickly thought that there were still one or two things which she wanted to finish.

Queen Victoria may have been withdrawn from the world, but she had all the love of life of her Hanoverian ancestors. She had a long experience of human nature, and a close knowledge of mankind derived from the management of her family and the court. Moreover, she naturally derived a great deal of information about what was afoot and what people were thinking from the members of her Court. Gladstone once said that he had a very bad opinion of Court gossip: it was "absolutely irresponsible" but is yet "uniformly admitted as infallible".[144] He was wrong. The Queen was perfectly capable of winnowing the false from the true. She was very adroit at avoiding an unwelcome topic of conversation. Her private secretary noticed that when someone at dinner started a subject of which the Queen disapproved she suddenly switched the conversation on to beef and cutlets. On another occasion one of her daughters asked an unfortunate question and the Queen turned it aside by saying, "Don't you think Lady Cunyngham so like the late Lord Hardinge?"[145]

Naturally enough the Queen was influenced by her position and her surroundings, but it is unjust to imply that she was swayed by the tittle-tattle of courts. In fact courtiers and secretaries alike were always complaining that she was impossible to influence. Reading those parts of her published correspondence, which cover the ten or twelve years of her seclusion, any impartial judge (though smiling at her displays of obstinacy

[144]John Morley, *Gladstone*, vol. II, p. 254. Gladstone was referring to the unaccountable hostility of the Queen to Lord Clarendon when he was forming his government in 1868. We now know, although Mr. Gladstone did not, that Clarendon was a brilliant and satirical gossip about the Queen, her family and the Court. No doubt this had come back to her and more than justified her wish to exclude Clarendon. The reader is referred to *My Dear Duchess*, edited by A. L. Kennedy, 1956.

[145]These, with many other delightful anecdotes about the Queen, will be found in Sir Henry Ponsonby's life by his son, Arthur Ponsonby, published in 1942.

and occasional childishness) is struck not only by the sound sense but by the good feeling which she brought to bear on the large problems by which she was faced. Through all her sighing and grumbling she worked without flagging: this saved her from thinking only of her misery, and as the country adjusted itself to see the Queen in her new setting, it came to realise the devotion, the strength of character and the rectitude which inspired the Queen.

IV

As we glance at the latest phase of the Queen's life—the last quarter during which she was acclaimed and during which she celebrated the triumphs of her jubilees—we become conscious of a softening in her character. She was grateful for the kindness and affection shown her: she was less petulant at the strokes of fate: and as she grew older her graces increased with no diminution of her authority. Her character was too robust and her experiences too varied to justify any comparison with the ladies of Cranford: but she had both the dignity and simplicity which we associate with the elderly ladies of Mrs. Gaskell's imagining. And it was unquestionably popularity that emphasised and disclosed the more agreeable side of her character. Circumstances had softened her and above all she was heartened by knowing that she was appreciated: it gave her confidence. After her jubilee in 1887 she wrote to Lord Rosebery explaining how "deeply and immensely" she had been touched by her reception; she added: "it shows that fifty years' *hard* work, anxiety and care have been appreciated".[146] Popularity and the softening shades of old age reveal her charm. In some ways this becomes more conspicuous to posterity than to her contemporaries: to them she was inevitably aloof and partially concealed, to us her private character is revealed by the publication of her correspondence and extracts from her journal. Looking through the closing volumes of the great

[146]*Letters*, Third Series, vol. 1, p. 341.

QUEEN ADELAIDE
*Detail from the
portrait by
Sir William Beechey*

KING WILLIAM IV
*Detail from the
portrait by
Sir David Wilkie*

QUEEN VICTORIA, 18
From a vignette by
Sir Edwin Landseer

PRINCESS VICTORIA,
AGED 15, WITH THE
DUCHESS OF KENT
From a vignette by
R. J. Lane after
George Hayter

H.M. QUEEN VICTORIA, 1841
*From the drawing by H. E. Dawe
at Buckingham Palace*

SILVER CROWN COIN
OF QUEEN VICTORIA
by W. Wyon

QUEEN AND PRINCE, 1854

BALMORAL CASTLE

*Both from Queen Victoria's "Leaves from the Journal
of Our Life in the Highlands", 1868*

OSBORNE HOUSE

QUEEN VICTORIA AND HER FAMILY, 1887
From the painting by S. Tuxen

THE QUEEN, PRINCESS LOUISE AND
JOHN BROWN, OSBORNE, 1865

QUEEN VICTORIA IN LATER LIFE

PRINCE AND PRINCESS OF WALES WITH
THEIR CHILDREN, 1880

PRINCE OF WALES, 1875

KING EDWARD VII

A FAMILY AND IMPERIAL GROUP AT COBURG, 1894
Back Row: Duke of Connaught, Duke of Saxe-Coburg, Emperor of Germany, Prince of Wales. In Front: The Queen and Empress Frederick

DUKE OF YORK, 1893

KING GEORGE V
ENTERING HYDE PARK
ABOUT 1930

KING GEORGE V
AT COWES, 1935

series of her letters we realise that we get to know the Queen more closely than is possible with any other of our Kings or Queens.

If Queen Victoria's journal could ever have been published in full we should possess not only a marvellous record of the nineteenth century but a revelation of human character which would rank with the great diarists—with Pepys, with Fanny Burney or with Parson Woodforde. Although the Queen was not a stylish writer—the lady novelist Ouida called the published extracts from her journal "silly" and "bad English"— she had a pre-eminent quality in any writer—the capacity to show her own feelings and to reveal herself through any episode she was describing. Nor did age dim this quality. Latterly she had to dictate the journal because of difficulty with her sight, but the account she gives of hearing of the death of her second son in the summer before her own death has all the feeling and dramatic instinct which we associate with her style at its zenith. "Osborne, 31 July 1900. A terrible day! When I had hardly finishing dressing, Lenchen [Princess Helena, her third daughter] and Beatrice [her youngest daughter] knocked at the door and came in. I at once asked whether there were any news, and Lenchen replied, 'Yes, bad news, very bad news: he has slept away.' Oh God! my poor darling Affie gone too! My third grown-up child, besides three very dear sons-in-law. It is hard at eighty-one!... I was greatly upset, one sorrow, one trial, one anxiety following another.... I pray God to help me to be patient and have trust in Him, who has never failed me!... Later Beatrice read to me in my room out of some of my favourite religious books, which was soothing.... It was most impressive hearing the minute guns being fired by the *Australia,* which had come round Osborne Bay for that purpose."

If she could rise to heights over a personal tragedy, she could likewise give graphic description of episodes which were trifling. Here is an account of a plague of frogs which she noticed at Frogmore. (In the summer, as there was no garden round Windsor Castle, the Queen very often spent the day at

Frogmore with her official work.) "28 June 1875. Rainy morning, but we went down all the same to Frogmore, and breakfasted in the Garden Cottage. We noticed an immense number of little frogs, hardly bigger than a blue-bottle fly, hopping and crawling all over the grass paths, which seemed to increase. I observed it first, yesterday, but much more to-day, and especially near the Cottage—quite disgusting." She went back to the Castle to hold a Council and then returned to Frogmore for tea "when the frogs were quite dreadful, making the grass look as if it were alive ! The paths had to be swept over and over again." A naturalist was then summoned to advise her and the Queen wrote that he told her that "frogs had come from all parts to breed in my beautiful piece of water: that the season had probably favoured this, and that the absence of ducks had let the spawn come to maturity. At the spawning time the eggs ought to be collected and put away, and the old frogs and toads destroyed, though a few were very valuable."

The vigour of her writing always came out on questions which stirred her feelings. In 1886 she drew up a memorandum about cruelty to animals—"As regards her poor dear friends the dogs, she would repeat that *no* dogs should ever be *killed* by *police unless* the veterinary surgeon declared they were mad. That dogs who were close to their masters or mistresses or their house-door, poor quiet dogs should be left alone and not molested. No dog should be *killed* till it is certain he *is* mad. *Fits are no* proof of *this*."

Her writing, as she grew older, lost nothing of its edge. She generally conveyed her disagreement or displeasure concentrated on the person in question, though she sometimes enjoyed giving it a wider range. When her Prime Minister complained that the Dean of Windsor, whose promotion in the Church was being urged by the Queen, was unknown, the Queen replied: "It is a complete error that the Dean of Windsor is not known. He is better known than most clergymen are."[147]

To the last her prejudices were unabated. Her dislike of Gladstone increased markedly with the years. She once wrote to a confidential friend that Disraeli's mind was "so much

[147] *Letters,* Third Series, vol. 1, p. 647.

greater, larger and his apprehension of things great and small so much quicker than that of Mr. Gladstone".[148] This was not really true but we can see, easily enough, how she came to believe it was. Disraeli, with a cunning which was rather jesuitical, contrived to give the Queen the impression that he and she were, between them, managing the affairs of the nation. Gladstone on the other hand seemed close and secretive, long-winded and hesitant—especially about things on which the Queen felt strongly. At a garden party in the summer of 1877 Disraeli came up to the Queen, when he was Prime Minister, bowed and said: "The crisis has begun and I shall need all your Majesty's support."[149] It was make-believe to which Gladstone's imagination could not rise or his truthfulness sink. But its effect on the Queen was magical. Again Disraeli's methods are illustrated by one of those personal questions—not perhaps of great importance but invariably agitating to Downing Street and Buckingham Palace. When Temple, headmaster of Rugby, was made a bishop, the governing body of the school appointed as headmaster Dr. Hayman. A reactionary, he speedily floundered in the Liberal environment of Dr. Arnold's Rugby. After four years he was dismissed by the Governors not for any incapacity but for political obduracy. The Queen described him as "totally unfit" to be headmaster,[150] and Disraeli had to try to solace the unhappy doctor with a Crown living, and to persuade the Queen to agree to the appointment. Gladstone would have delved minutely into all the circumstances and personal issues. Disraeli began by saying that: "your Majesty has sometimes deigned to assist Mr. Disraeli with your Counsel" and how enormously he valued her "almost unrivalled experience of public life". He closed his letter with a reference to this unfortunate gentleman, "who next week will have to leave Rugby, with nine children, absolutely homeless and shelterless".[151]

Much has been written of the Queen's relations with Glad-

[148]Ibid., Second Series, vol. II, p. 428.
[149]Ibid., p. 547.
[150]Ibid., p. 334.
[151]Ibid., p. 334. See also James M. Wilson, An Autobiography, 1836-1931.

stone.[152] But two points may even now be fairly emphasised. Although the Queen disliked Gladstone and was never at ease with him, the reasons for her distrust of him were political and not personal. In the second half of the 1870's and inspired by the highest moral motives Gladstone had roused the country against Disraeli's Eastern policy, which had seemed to condone Turkish misrule: he called up the same sort of wild, unreasoning storm which had swept Walpole out of office 130 years earlier. This was what the Queen could not forgive. In 1879 she expressed her views for transmission to the Liberal leaders: she stated categorically: "I never could take Mr. Gladstone as my minister again, for I never COULD have the slightest *particle* of confidence in Mr. Gladstone *after* his violent, mischievous and dangerous conduct for the last three years."[153]

She had of course to swallow these words. In some ways she did this with a bad grace. Her personal behaviour to him—especially over General Gordon—was intolerable, but yet she did fight her prejudices, and struggled to remember that—however uncongenial he may have been—they both had a responsibility to the public. In this connexion the Queen's cautionary language—often overlooked in the violence of some of her outbursts—should be remembered in her favour. At the beginning of 1883 she wrote: "The Queen is sure that Mr. Gladstone will not misunderstand her, when she expresses her earnest hopes that he will be very guarded in his language when he goes to Scotland shortly, and that he will remember the immense importance attached to *every* word falling from him. Words spoken are often the cause of difficulty hereafter."[154] Although much sympathy has been lavished on Gladstone, such feelings should be tempered by an understanding of the difficulties of the Queen, who sincerely felt that the gifts and personality of the statesman gave him a majority, which he used to impose policies on the country which it did not want. To a ducal supporter of the Liberals she wrote of her difficulties

---

[152]See the excellent biography of Gladstone by Sir Philip Magnus.
[153]*Letters*, Second Series, vol. II, p. 48.
[154]*Letters*, Second Series, vol. III, p. 395.

with Gladstone: "You will feel for me, who am greatly, I think, to be pitied. I cannot do the good I wish, or prevent the evil I see."[155]

And in that sense of frustration lay the explanation for some of her indiscretions—political partisanship which would be thought grossly unconstitutional to-day. Possibly the outstanding example of this was her *"very secret"* letter to Lord Beaconsfield after he had been succeeded in the premiership by Gladstone in 1880. The letter was signed "Ever yours affectionately" and included the statement: "I *never* write except on formal *official* matters to the Prime Minister" and "I look always to *you* for ultimate help. But I take care that they *know* what I *think*." Hardly less extraordinary was her advice to Lord Rosebery, when he became Foreign Secretary, in 1886, that he should—so far as foreign affairs were concerned—bring them as little as possible before the cabinet "where nothing is decided."[156]

In her political opinions Queen Victoria was certainly not a Conservative. With opinions which were at that time the foundation of Conservatism—resistance to change, veneration for the Church and national institutions and the preservation of the squirearchy she had no real sympathy. The Queen always maintained that her politics were progressive—"Liberal as she has ever been"[157] were her own words—but where she parted with the Liberals was in her ideas of Empire. Although she would not have liked the label she was a Chamberlainite, a Kiplingite, an imperialist of the new school which drew her— in spite of herself—into the Conservative camp.

And as she grew older her mind ranged freely over the affairs of her people and in all kinds of trivial matters she showed how naturally a practical or common-sense mind drifts out of sympathy with progressive thought. In the closing years of the nineteenth century there was some very proper agitation against the liquor trade, and the Liberal Party came into pos-

[155]*Ibid.*, Second Series, vol. III, p. 548.
[156]*Ibid.*, Third Series, vol. I, p. 48.
[157]*Ibid.*, Second Series, vol. III, p. 73.

session of a sizable temperance following. In 1880 the Queen wrote to Gladstone lamenting a proposed tax on beer because it was unjust to tax the drink of the poor and not the wine of the rich. "The poor never drink wine", she wrote—a fact of which we may assume Mr. Gladstone to have been well aware.[158] She added that the rich wine-drinker was not restrained in his indulgences. When "More Leaves From the Journal of a Life in the Highlands" was in preparation some advisers thought it might be wise to leave out references to the rather frequent toast-bibbing by the Highlanders. The Queen swept this suggestion to one side: she could see no point in the omission "except to please the total abstinence movement,"[159] On another occasion she only consented to the appointment of a particular cleric to a canonry at Westminster if he agreed, when preaching in the Abbey, not to use "the very strong total abstinence language which he has carried to such an extreme hitherto,"[160]

On questions of "publicity" the Queen naturally had strong views. Anything concerning her "private, domestic life" was excluded from the newspapers, magazine articles or books,[161] though she evidently contemplated that anecdotes about her private life would be accessible after her death. During her reign everything which the public had a right to know about the Queen was in the Court Circular, which was occasionally enlivened by a passage from the Queen's pen. Her feelings over the death of some foreign royalty, some courtier or a faithful servant were often set out in her own inimitable style.

A characteristic example is the account of the death of Sir Howard Elphinstone in March 1890 in the Court Circular:

The Queen received yesterday with profound grief the terrible news of the untimely death of Sir Howard Elphinstone. Sir Howard enjoyed Her Majesty's entire confidence, esteem and friendship for thirty-one years, and had been

158*Letters*, Second Series, vol. III, p. 114.
159*Ibid*., p. 445.
160*Ibid*., Third Series, vol. I, p. 359.
161See the Preface to Mrs. Gerald Gurney, *The Childhood of Queen Victoria*, 1901.

selected by the Prince Consort as Governor to H.R.H. the
Duke of Connaught when the Prince was only eight and a
half.

The lamented General who was a very distinguished
officer and most accomplished man, visited Her Majesty
on the 6th at Windsor and took leave of the Queen on the
morning of the 7th, having told her that he would be back
in England in three weeks!

All the Royal Family unite with the Queen in deeply
deploring Sir H. Elphinstone's loss—as he was greatly
respected and beloved by all of them.

At the beginning of the 1890's the *Daily Telegraph* strongly
urged that newspapers should be given more news about the
Queen. She simply minuted the suggestion for her private
secretary's guidance in replying "The Queen strongly objects
to this. The Court Circular is ample."[162]

To death duties her resistance was possibly inevitable: "the
fatal Death Rates", as she described them in a letter to her
Prime Minister. The reasons for her objections were characteristic. She thought that country houses would become unoccupied,
and she thought the duties would impose suffering on widows:
she told the Chancellor of the Exchequer that she had always
deplored the minute examination of a widow's possessions, at
the moment of anguish, by probate officials.[163]

The picture of the Queen would be ill-proportioned if the
impression were left that her comments were confined to political issues: they ranged widely over many aspects of the nation's
life. At the end of the nineteenth century one of the popular
forms of baiting Roman Catholics lay in the suggestion that
terrible horrors were concealed by the enclosed orders for
women, and that convents should be open to inspection by the
state. The Queen, at the close of her life, grew uneasy on this
topic and asked the Duke of Norfolk to write a memorandum
for her on these possible dangers. He explained to her both the
arrangements prevailing and the type of lady entering the con-

[162]*Letters,* Third Series, vol. II, p. 71.
[163]A. G. Gardiner, *Sir William Harcourt,* vol. II, p. 298.

vent and told the Queen bluntly that talk of inspection or state controls of convents was deeply wounding to Roman Catholics. The Queen thanked him for his trouble, and assured him that she was much more comfortable and reassured.[164]

Her respect for human life was strong, and anything which seemed to imperil existence needlessly, roused her annoyance. Her preoccupation with recklessness on the railways is an indication of this, as was her dislike for expeditions in search of the Pole. "She hopes it will *not* be encouraged" was her comment on the Government-financed expedition to the North Pole in the 1870's under Admiral Nares. Occasionally her observations were coloured more by temper than by reason. She thought that education ruined the health of the higher classes and made the working classes unfit to be good servants and labourers. When Lady Amberley—daughter-in-law of her former Prime Minister John Russell—made a speech in favour of women having the vote the Queen commented "she ought to get a good whipping".[165] Of the *Greville Memoirs* (now generally accepted as the first authority for the political history of the nineteenth century) she wrote "that horrible book".[166]

Occasionally she turned, with this same kind of severity, on her ministers. In 1878, Lord Carnarvon, who was Colonial Secretary in Disraeli's government, in replying to a commercial deputation, spoke critically of the Government's foreign policy, especially its apparent bolstering up of the Turk. The Queen wrote to Carnarvon to express her "deep concern" that he should have allowed his personal feelings "which she is bound to say SHE *cannot* understand" to find vent in "a speech to a commercial deputation. . . . It is (the Queen must speak *strongly*) lamentable!" She ended by saying that nothing gave her more pain than seeing people "for whom she had a *sincere regard*" take a view of foreign affairs which seemed to her "*most* detrimental to the position of her great Empire". This must have been an uncomfortable letter to receive, and we are hardly surprised that Lord Carnarvon thought it best to lay

[164]*Letters*, Third Series, vol. III, p. 233.
[165]Sir T. Martin, *Queen Victoria as I Knew Her*.
[166]*Letters*, Second Series, vol. II, p. 372–8.

down his office.[167] Four years later Gladstone was about to include the then Lord Derby in his cabinet, who had been a Conservative but like Lord Carnarvon could not follow that party's
foreign policy; Derby made a speech at Manchester, in which
he had said that the British should not stay in Egypt a day
longer than was necessary to restore order; the Queen sent Gladstone a copy of the speech with the comment: "Mr. Gladstone
will introduce a most disagreeable and irresolute, timid Minister
into his cabinet, if he really offers Lord Derby a place in it."[168]
Three days before this letter Gladstone had had an interview
with the Queen at which he told her of his intention to
include Derby, "Most difficult ground" was his comment, and
he added that they got over it "aided by her beautiful manners".[169] Derby became Colonial Secretary a few days later.[170] And
the most stinging of her rebukes fell to the luckless Gladstone.
When Khartoum fell and General Gordon was killed he was
staying with Lord Hartington, in the lovely setting of Holker
in North Lancashire. The rustic post-master in the agreeable
little town of Cark-in-Cartmel must have been distinctly flus-
tered to take off a telegram from the Queen *en clair* which
contained the sentence: "To think that all this might have
been prevented and many precious lives saved by earlier action
is too frightful. V.R.I."[171] Gladstone is believed never to have
forgiven this public admonishment. Yet however much sympathy for Gladstone instinctively rises and indignation with
the Queen makes itself felt, we remember that the Queen's
anger sprang from patriotism. Though in the twentieth century such sentiments may seem as archaic as Jacobitism, she had
expressed her convictions to Disraeli some five years before
"we must, with our Indian Empire and large Colonies, be

[167]*Letters*, Second Series, vol. II, pp. 588-9.

[168]*Ibid.*, Second Series, vol. III, p. 378.

[169]Morley, *Life of Gladstone*, vol. III, p. 100

[170]Derby – the 15th Earl, 1826 to 1893 – was a curious product of a
great Conservative family. The Queen's suspicion of him primarily arose
because of his opposition to any further extension of the Empire. Graphi-
cally and possibly sensibly he expressed his feelings by saying: "We do
not want any more black men."

[171]*Letters*, Second Series, vol. II, p. 597.

prepared for attacks and wars, somewhere or other CONTINU-
ALLY. And the *true economy* will be *to be always ready*."[172] We
can perfectly understand how burdensome Gladstone—and indeed all ministers—found the stream of correspondence with the
Queen. A Conservative Prime Minister (Salisbury) amusingly
grumbled: "I could do very well with two departments; in fact
I have four—the Prime Ministership, the Foreign Office, the
Queen and Randolph Churchill." Salisbury, who made that
observation in a moment of exasperation, also said that the
Queen was full of consideration and concession: he might have
added "but not to Gladstone". For that was the measure of the
difference between her relations with Gladstone and her relations with the Conservatives.

And in considering these closing years of the Queen's life
the reader, as he turns over the pages of her correspondence
and notes the flashes of prejudice and temper, likewise notices
the marks of a personality which was as forceful as it was predictable. A scrupulous examination in no wise diminishes admiration. Although she may have been self-indulgent when her
feelings were concerned, she did not spare her physique. It is
perhaps surprising to learn that she often was at work at one
in the morning; she explained to Disraeli that she hardly ever
went to bed before one.[173] Her control over herself was inexorable.
In 1888 she had a brief important interview with Emperor
Francis Joseph—"I unfortunately had a very bad sick head-
ache." However, the British Ambassador in Vienna reported
that the Emperor was enchanted and that the general effect
of the meeting was quite excellent.[174] The Queen had revealed no trace of her discomfort.

Routine meant much to the Queen—perhaps principally because it saved time. She was meticulously punctual: if anyone
kept her waiting—even for a moment—she would ask: "How
am I to get through my day if I am kept waiting?" Any sudden alteration to the normal round of her life was unthink-
able. When Gladstone urged her, in 1885, to interrupt her stay

172*Letters*, Second Series, vol. III, p. 38.
173*Ibid.*, Second Series, vol. II, pp. 561–2.
174*Ibid.*, Third Series, vol. I, pp. 401, 409.

in Scotland to travel nearer to London owing to a threatened political crisis she excused herself on the grounds that the railway authorities thought it not safe for her to travel without some days' warning. And then she added what was, we may suspect, the real reason: "The Queen is a lady nearer seventy than sixty"; "her health has been severely taxed during her arduous reign"; "she could not rush about like a man or younger person."[175] But woman-like she was impatient of anything like formality or *amour propre* in others. When her own physician refused to see Lord Beaconsfield, who was dying, because a homoeopathist was in attendance, the Queen wrote to him, begged him to "waive this little professional difficulty" and added that any refusal "would be much felt by the country".[176]

Although her life may of necessity have been bounded by formality, part of the greatness of Queen Victoria lay in her capacity for allowing her own personality to rise triumphant above officialdom—above the prearranged programme. In the early days of the South African War she reviewed the Household Cavalry at Windsor. At the close of the ceremony the men came crowding round her carriage and she spoke to them in her clear, bell-like voice words of simplicity and affection which closed with the petition to God "to protect you and bring you back safely home". After the men had given their cheers for the Queen "they gave many more and would hardly stop".[177] The scene was spontaneous and memorable.

Her human sympathies were intensely strong and she was never inhibited from expressing them. Later sovereigns have been over-anxious that expressions of sorrow and sympathy should not run beyond the formal and well-tried channels. The Queen, on the other hand, never hesitated to write to strangers. A characteristic example is her letter to the widow of the British Resident at Cabul, Sir Pierre Cavagnari, who was murdered in 1879; the Queen opened: "Though I am a total stranger to you and never had the pleasure of knowing personally your distinguished and noble husband . . ." She went on: "It is

[175]*Letters*, Second Series, vol. III, p. 662.
[176]*Ibid.*, p. 206.　[177]*Journal*, 11 November 1899.

quite impossible for me to express what my feelings are or *how* my heart bleeds for you," and ended, "Yours truly and sympathisingly".[178] Though on occasions she was alarming to her own sons and daughters she was at her best—sympathetic and understanding—with her later descendants and indeed with all children. Lord Kilmarnock was horrified to find that one of his small sons had written to the Queen and that a servant had mistakenly posted the letter. He wrote forthwith to the Queen's private secretary to apologise. This was shown to the Queen, who minuted back to her secretary: "Pray tell Lord Kilmarnock that the Queen was delighted with the little letter as nothing pleases her more than the artless kindness of innocent children. She has written him an answer and has posted it to him."[179] Her feelings for children are also illustrated by her reply to an idiotic courtier who had asked if she had ever seen King George III. (She was nine months old when George III died.) "What, show a poor old madman to a sweet little baby!" were her indignant words, recalled by her grand-daughter Princess Marie Louise.

If she showed much sympathetic interest in those at the start of life, she also showed an absorbed fascination in the end of life. She liked to know every detail of the closing hours of friends and relatives, and death seems to hallow and muffle even her vivid and vital style of writing. "Dr. Reid came with the news of a terribly sad accident which has happened to dear Mrs. Prothero [wife of the Rector of the parish which included Osborne]. She has fallen out of the window and is *no more*."[180] When the Archbishop of Canterbury died suddenly while on a visit to Mr. Gladstone the Queen wrote: "What a beautiful thought that he almost passed away in church, while at his prayers!"[181] And when the widow of her private secretary died she wrote to a member of the family: "May I ask for the last photograph taken of her? and will you not have one taken

---

[178]*Letters*, Second Series. vol. III, p. 43.
[179]*Ibid.*, Third Series, vol. I, p. 228.
[180]*Ibid.*, Second Series, vol. II, p. 286.
[181]*Ibid.*, Third Series, vol. III, p. 93.

of her now, or a drawing?"[182] Occasionally her true self flashed
out even on these mournful occasions. When the Prince Consort's only brother died she recalled "the happy past . . . so many,
many things", and the dead man's "frequent visits formerly",
and then she added "though he was often very trying".[183] Indeed
he was.

Perhaps the last because it is the fairest memory of the Queen
at her life's end should rest with herself and her family circle.
Many comments exist to support the belief that Queen Victoria
was a Spartan mother and terrifying grandmother, administer-
ing snubs and reproofs, gliding into a room and withering a
group of her relations with a flash from those clear blue, promin-
ent Hanoverian eyes. Certainly where anything concerning the
dignity of the Crown or of the Royal Family was involved
she was adamant. Although her handling of her grandson—
the German Emperor—was masterly she did—on at least one
occasion—give him a stinging rebuke about the tone of a letter
which he had written to her. "I doubt"—she wrote— "whether
any Sovereign, ever wrote in such terms to another Sovereign
and that Sovereign his grandmother. . . . I never should do
such a thing . . . your visit to *Osborne not to Cowes* I looked on
as a visit for my birthday. . . . Always your very affectionate
Grandmother V.R.I."[184] Descending from this imperial stage
to the level of more ordinary mortals we find her saying to a
daughter of the Belgian Royal House: "You must dress your
hair differently, and in a manner more suitable to a Princess."[185]
But if she expected much out of respect to the station to which
she belonged she was the first to do honour to those of her
children who, like herself, were, as the royal books of reference
express it, *majesté* or rulers. In describing her jubilee procession

[182]*Letters,* Third Series, vol. I, p. 352.

[183]*Ibid.,* Third Series, vol. II, p. 305.

[184]*Ibid.,* Third Series, vol. III, p. 382. The Queen's correction about
Cowes is a reproof. The Emperor, who loved the yacht racing at Cowes,
evidently loosely referred to visiting Cowes: the Queen reminds him
that the visit is not for the gaieties of Cowes but to the seclusion of his
grandmother's home.

[185]The Princess Louise of Belgium, *My Own Affairs,* 1921.

of 1897 she explains that she had to sit by herself on the seat of the carriage facing the horses. The Empress Frederick could not in consequence travel in the same carriage with the Queen because "her rank as Empress prevented her sitting with her back to the horses".[186] When her second son, shortly after his succession as reigning Duke of Saxe-Coburg-Gotha, came to visit her at Balmoral she writes in her Journal: "I met him at the door in the Hall." The point of her saying this is that it was a customary civility for a visiting ruler to be met at the door: even though the visitor was her own son the full formalities had to be maintained.

In her published correspondence there are, as is well known, many instances of her expressing herself sharply and disagreeably to her children in letters. She strongly disapproved of many things done by her eldest son, the Prince of Wales, his racing, his social gaieties, his general air of restlessness, "The Country and all of *us* would like to see you a little more stationary"[187] is a characteristic reproof in one of her letters. In 1870 the Prince wrote to the Queen: "I fear, dear Mama, that no year goes round without your giving me a jobation[188] on the subject of racing." But she never hesitated to express her annoyance when he did anything of which she disapproved, whether it was over his friendship with Lord Randolph Churchill or the neglect which he was thought to have shown to "the naturally sensitive and warm-hearted people of Wales". Yet in an official family such as her own she had learned from the Prince Consort that the wisest course was to put on paper subjects of discord and matters in dispute. The Queen showed her wisdom in doing this rather than in having disagreeable wrangles and discussions face to face. But the squabbles, through being committed to paper, have survived while the more peaceful personal relationships which they fostered have vanished with all the rest of the Victorian glories. There are, however, some surviving indications to suggest that the Queen, as mother and grand-

186*Letters*, Third Series, vol. III, p. 175.

187*Ibid.*, Second Series, vol. I, p. 369.

188Dialect for jawing—not perhaps a very wise word to use to the Queen. *Letters*, Second Series, vol. II, p. 19.

mother, was far more sympathetic and affectionate than is some-times supposed. Her daughters, especially the youngest, Princess Beatrice, were her constant companions. "This darling child— my blessing and comfort" was the Queen's description of her. In 1878 when the Princess was twenty-one the Royal Family had a little impromptu dance in the Drawing Room at Osborne and even after eighty years we can catch the awe of the on-lookers as they realised that, out of respect to her daughter, the Queen was dancing: she was valsing, which she had not done since the death of the Prince Consort "and I found I could do it as well as ever".[189]

No doubt some of the Queen's children felt that the younger princesses—Beatrice and Helena—engrossed too much of their mother. "The harem of Princesses", as they were sometimes loosely and rudely called in the more masculine circles which surrounded the Prince of Wales, must have been at times an irritant. But penetrating these custodians the elder children found their mother's charm and devotion undiminished. There are several references in her journal to the Prince of Wales's kindness to her and how greatly she enjoyed his visits alone to Balmoral: "It was very dear and kind of him to come all that way to see me, for only two days, and gave me great pleasure."[190] Her relationship with her daughter-in-law, the Princess of Wales, was one of deep affection on each side. The Princess was not afraid of the Queen: on occasions without making friction she stood up to the Queen, especially over matters affecting the upbringing of her sons. Their affection and respect for one another—so different from the squabbles of the earlier genera-tion of the Royal Family—are illustrated by the Princess's letter to the Queen, written after she had been married for fifteen years: "Many, many thanks for your most affectionate letter on my birthday with all the kind things you say of me; but I really feel quite ashamed of so much praise as I don't deserve a quarter of it, though one thing at least is true—how entirely I return your affection, which I value above all things."[191]

[189]*Letters*, Second Series, vol. II, p. 616.
[190]*Ibid.*, Third Series, vol. I, p. 443.
[191]*Ibid.*, Second Series, vol. II, p. 469.

To her grandson, the Duke of Clarence, who was possibly a rather difficult member of the family, she had always shown affectionate understanding: it is believed that she was even prepared to consider his renouncing the throne in order to marry a Roman Catholic princess. After the Duke's untimely death, when he was twenty-eight, his father wrote to the Queen: "You were, dearest Mama, always very kind to him and fond of him, which he greatly appreciated." And the Queen adds: "I truly did love and understand the darling boy."[192]

At the end of her long life—she died in her eighty-second year—she could look with pride on her descendants. They filled or were about to fill the thrones of Europe: they carried the distinguished tradition of Victoria and Albert to the Empires of Germany and Russia, to the Kingdoms of Greece and Roumania and later to those of Norway and Spain: as well as to countless duchies and dynasties in the heart of Germany. As we turn to those great family gatherings which she loved, and look perhaps on the picture of the Queen and her descendants painted for the Jubilee of 1887 and see the gay uniforms and the long, shrewd Coburg faces we become conscious of an international force which was powerful so long as the central figure lived to keep it together and might—if the conditions of the nineteenth-century had lasted longer—have proved an abiding influence in the fortunes of Europe. Of that she herself was not unmindful. But whatever their might and grandeur they remained, always in her eyes, her own devoted family. She showed this in her account of what she felt when her granddaughter married the Emperor of Russia in 1894. This granddaughter, owing to the premature death of her own mother Princess Alice, had been much with the Queen in girlhood. The Queen gave a large dinner in honour of the wedding, and rose to give the toast: "I wish to propose the healths of the Emperor and Empress of Russia, my dear grandchildren." She adds in her journal: "How I thought of darling Alicky, and how impossible it seemed that that gentle little simple Alicky should be the great Empress of Russia."[193]

[192]Letters, Third Series, vol. II, p. 93.
[193]Ibid., p. 454.

And when at length the Queen died at Osborne at half-past six in the evening on 22 January 1901, she breathed her last, in the words of the official bulletin "surrounded by her children and grandchildren". And the last words which she was heard consciously to form was the family name of her eldest son—"Bertie".

CHAPTER III

EDWARD VII

Of the four sovereigns in this book the one to whom history has not been kind is King Edward VII. There are particular reasons for this, though it is likely that as we move further from his age he may fall back into something nearer his rightful place. The chief reason for the King's diminished reputation in the middle of the twentieth-century is that although the reading public is avidly curious about the Edwardian Age the characteristics of the people of that time are antipathetic to us. Books of reminiscences, together with sketchy histories of that golden epoch, have been among the most popular reading of the last ten or fifteen years. We seem to be carried backwards by such books to a world, heavy with good things—the finest Havana cigars, the best champagne, the plumpest quails, the stateliest women moving through large living-rooms sweet with the smell of countless tuberoses, and in the background the heart-melting lilt of *The Merry Widow*.[1] The country was rich, and those who had the spending of the national wealth did so with enjoyment, with ostentation, with gusto and—as our purists of the twentieth century love to remind us—with a touch of vulgarity. From the more meagre world of the 1950's we enjoy picturing for ourselves this now long-distant age—a time when everything seemed a shade larger than life, a world of groaning tables, brimming glasses and prodigious men-servants. Perhaps inevitably the picture is tinged with envy of those who lived surrounded by all these delights and accepted them as a right, as a part of inheritance. The Edwardians somewhat resembled that nobleman who finding that he was missing everything out shooting suddenly addressed the Almighty: "Oh, God, you know how I love shooting. Why won't You let me hit any birds today?" They were in fact a shade spoiled.

[1] King Edward first saw *The Merry Widow* in Vienna and urged George Edwardes to produce it in London. See Lord Esher, *Journal*, vol. II, p. 272.

To us the most spoiled and the most self-indulgent of that social circle is naturally its leader who, as Prince of Wales and King for half a century, marked society with his self-indulgence and high spirits. "Guttural and gluttonous Bertie" were the words, given prominence in one of the expensive Sunday newspapers, to portray the King in a nutshell. Though we can understand the reaction which gives rise to that outburst, we should in justice temper our indignation against the King by two reflections. Extravagant living at that time was not the exclusive privilege of the English: their habits were almost frugal in contrast with those of the Viennese, and if in imagination we cross the Atlantic and settle round the massive mahogany at the house of the great Vanderbilt hostess "Alice of the Breakers" we shall realise at once that rich food and drink were not to be found only at Marlborough House. The other point to notice is that "gluttony" was by no means confined to one class in England. The middle and professional classes set the greatest store by "a good table". Here is a typical menu for a private household in the 1860's: 2 soups, 10 kinds of fish, 4 entrées, 6 hot joints, 4 cold birds, 7 sweets, dessert and ices.[2] Although it is true that the majority of people were denied these pleasures, the favourite and most popular form of charity at that time was a free dinner with unlimited rounds of beef and unlimited plum pudding. But whatever may be said in palliation of their habits, the fact remains that the self-indulgence of the later Victorians and Edwardians is a barrier between us and them. With their vanities and frivolities they seem to belong to some species of proud, resplendent bird. "The old peacock" was indeed a phrase used by the Emperor William to describe his uncle—King Edward. But in the case of the King at any rate, behind all the plumage and display, was there not in reality a human-being, and a sovereign as widely loved as his mother but loved with less awe and more personal affection?

In addition to the now general reaction against the leading Edwardian personalities there are particular reasons why King Edward's stock stands low. There are three.

In 1912, very soon after the death of the King which took

[2] Arnold Palmer, *Movable Feasts*, 1952.

place in May 1910, the *Dictionary of National Biography* published a hasty and somewhat unfriendly account of the King. The article was written by Sidney Lee, a Shakespearian scholar, and its tone can be gauged from such phrases as : "he was unremitting in his devotion to social pleasures", in home politics "he was content with the role of onlooker", and that he showed "a certain disinclination to adapt his private plans to political emergencies". This article, at once airy and authoritative, caused disquiet to the King's family and friends and amply justified those who dismissed the King as a *flâneur* and those who rail against him for being lazy. The article was a hasty judgement, but the Dictionary in which it appeared seemed to give it credit and finality. The matter was not improved by an invitation to the writer of the article to undertake the King's official biography.

Secondly, those who have hurried to the defence of the King have attempted to magnify his position and to put him (as it were) in too large a frame. To argue that he was an international statesman with the capacity of a Bismarck or the foresight of a Cavour is absurd and does his reputation little good. With certain undeniable gifts of a statesman (though not all) and with power which was really negligible he yet accomplished much. That was the achievement of the King, but except for one perceptive writer[3] it never seems to have been squarely stated.

Thirdly, the King was not gifted with any capacity to express himself on paper. His letters were dashed off in a flowing, illegible hand—their subject-matter pleasant, conventional and banal. The editor of his mother's letters (Lord Esher) was undeniably right when he said "the truest service to the Queen is to let her speak for herself". But that is certainly not the truest service to the King, though it was mistakenly attempted in his official biography. The King perhaps only revealed his true quality—his wit and spirit—with his circle of private friends. Sportsmen, rich lords and men of pleasure, they were not capable of recording for posterity King Edward as he really was. Outside their intimate circle kings and princes are rightly

[3]F. J. C. Hearnshaw, *Edwardian England*, 1933.

constrained in what they say, and from the scraps which have come down to us it is not perhaps easy to piece together the attributes of King Edward which made him at the time our most popular king. For the reasons given above a curtain has fallen between ourselves and this gay, amusing, volatile prince, and it is the purpose of this sketch to attempt to draw aside the curtain, and to observe him rather more as he struck his contemporaries.

King Edward was born on 9 November 1841—one of our few rulers to be heir to the throne from the moment of his birth. He was baptised in St. George's Chapel, Windsor, in the following January when he was given—not the customary string of royal names but only two—Albert after his father and Edward after Queen Victoria's father. There were great rejoicings, and in London his initials, illuminated, were on many buildings. A sardonic wit remarked "It will be lucky for us if he is not soon acquainted with the three other vowels I.O.U." He was known in the family circle as Bertie but for official purposes he was invariably known by both his christian names, according to the nineteenth-century fashion of Louis Philippe, Victor Emanuel, Frederick William or Francis Joseph.

As a child he was very small. With fair hair and the bright complexion of his mother he was a pretty boy, and this appearance was enhanced by a taking manner and winning ways. His personality was the exact opposite of his mother and father; they were guarded – the Queen from shyness the Prince Consort from discretion. Their son loved, even as a child, chat and gossip. He is supposed to have asked the great Archbishop of Canterbury (Howley), who was the last of the bishops to wear the wig, "Whatever is that you've got on your head?" This kind of indiscreet question and comment was anathema to his parents—though it may well have been a trait inherited from George III. Both parents were severe with him—the Queen because she was terrified lest the child should be spoiled by the obsequiousness and flattery of Court life, the Prince in the hope of guiding his mind into the serious preoccupations which absorbed his own intellect. Deeply affectionate, the boy was devoted to his father and mother though he feared them. But

the easy family relationships of the twentieth century should
not blind us to the fact that Victorian parents in all walks of
life were formidable rather than demonstrative, unfriendly and
with words of restraint rather than endearment springing to
their lips. In that respect the Prince's home life was characteristic of his generation.

The education of this affectionate and sympathetic boy was
—as all the world knows—terrifying. Tutors, curricula, syl-
labuses, interminable lessons occupied his life (though not his
mind) from the age of seven. He learned something, though
not much. When his father and the advisers of the Royal Family
were drawing up the plans for the education of the Prince
they defined their objective, simply but bravely, as follows:
"The great object in view is to make him the most perfect
man." There we seem to catch in those contemporaries of
Dr. Arnold and Samuel Butler (the great headmaster of Shrews-
bury) something of the glad confidence in education felt by the
thinkers of the nineteenth century. If those who framed the
educational programme for the Prince lived to see the result of
their labours they may themselves have learned one thing from
it—the truth of a saying of Lord Melbourne about education:
"It may mould and direct character but it rarely alters it."
When his education was grinding to its end, the Prince Consort
wrote to his brother with this comment about the Prince: "He
has no interest for things but all the more for persons." The
Prince Consort shrewdly added that this trait was characteristic
of the English Royal Family, and that it was one of the reasons
why they were so popular. But he added that it greatly encouraged "small-talk".[4] The Prince Consort would have warmly
echoed that famous precept "Servants talk about people: gentlefolk discuss things."

So the Prince emerged from the savagery of the Victorian
schoolroom—unlearned but unspoiled. In company he was
cheerful, easy and agreeable—gracing each occasion with a
memorably charming smile and a beautifully articulated voice.
(Not the smallest of the services of the ancient university of

[4]*The Prince Consort And His Brother*, edited by Hector Bolitho, 1933.

Oxford was to rub off the harsher notes of his German accent.) Although his Hanoverian temper could blaze on occasions he was by nature extremely pleasant, anxious to be liked and to put people at their ease. His good nature is suggested by the fact that although, in later life, he often amused his contemporaries with tales of the educational chamber of horrors from which he emerged he never attacked his parents or railed against them.

Some of his contemporaries, attempting to excuse the later extravagances of his life, have perhaps exaggerated the severity of his father's system. When he left the world of home lessons and private tutors he was eighteen, and he was sent to Oxford. Certainly he was somewhat hedged in by equerries and dons, but at the end of his first term he said that he had never been so happy in his life.[5] He charmed the dons and their wives with his graceful manners: at dinner parties it was noticed that he did not follow the vulgar fashion of escorting his hostess arm-in-arm but rather walked deferentially behind her. He delighted the stout-hearted Anglican dons by laughing at the absurdities of Roman Catholics, and with characteristic indiscretion he introduced them to the larger world of European royalty with the news that his mother's cousin, the King of Hanover, was completely governed by his barber.[6]

While he was still at Oxford he carried out an important tour of Canada, and then moved on to the United States un-officially as Lord Renfrew. He was accompanied by the royal enclosure of officialdom which is customary on those occasions. Among his advisers was the Secretary of State for the Colonies —that Jonah, the Duke of Newcastle, as he was rather cruelly called at the time[7]—and the Duke reported back to the boy's parents rather in the style of a headmaster. Another of the suite, in similar vein, told the Queen: "H.R.H. seems pleased with everything, himself included." The King of the Belgians was

[5] *Diary of an Oxford Lady*: 1843–1862, 1932.   [6] *Ibid.*
[7] *Life and Letters of 4th Earl of Clarendon*. The Duke was an unlucky man. His wife bolted from him to marry an obscure Belgian. His conduct of the War office during the Crimean War nearly brought the nation to its knees.

rightly enthusiastic about the young Prince's part in what he called "this tremendous tour". The President of the United States told the Queen that the tour had been "a trying ordeal" for a person of the Prince's age, and he added how greatly the American people had been touched by the Prince's frankness, affability and dignity. The British Minister at Washington reported to the Queen how he had been struck by the tact and judgement he had shown in his dealings with the American people. Advice from the family, cautious restraint from courtiers, prudent words from Newcastle were no doubt valuable, but it was the Prince's handling of the unexpected which showed his mastery of the character of the New World. No doubt he was fully primed by his advisers when he accompanied the President to Mount Vernon, but confronted with the tombs with their majestic inscriptions "Washington" and "Martha—Consort of Washington", he seems spontaneously to have thought of asking to be allowed to plant a a chestnut, and bring others back to plant in Windsor Great Park. This was the conspicuous moment of the tour. Again no amount of coaching could have helped him when the ballroom, under the weight of several thousands of "the top people" of New York, collapsed. While an army of carpenters was at work he moved informally among the guests, but he had to confess to his mother that the evening was not a success for 5,000 came where 3,000 had been asked and it was very difficult to move.

His private letters home disappointed his parents. Certainly they were characteristically trite and banal. The cod fisheries, he told the Queen, were "the staple produce of St. John's, Newfoundland"; the harbour was "pretty and like Balaclava"; Washington is "a fine looking town and contains some striking buildings. The finest is the Capitol in which the Congress sits. All the Public Offices are in the same building." He ended his letter with the suggestion that: "We might easily take some hints for our own buildings which are so very bad." But if he was a little dull in describing what he saw, his characteristic thoughtfulness for others touched the Queen. He sent her a small piece of sweet briar which he thought she would like to

have from her father's ruined lodge in Nova Scotia, where he
had lived with his French mistress as a young man.

Yet in spite of emancipation across the Atlantic he continued
his syllabus of learning. On reaching England in November
he immediately returned to Oxford, and then in response to
that curious quirk of impartiality which too often neutralises
royalty he moved across to Cambridge—a period of his life
which was not happy and not successful. In the summer he
spent several weeks on the Curragh, attached to the 2nd Bat-
talion, Grenadier Guards. Although some of his attendants
were still hovering in the background, this was the first time
in his life that he was allowed to mix freely with his contemporaries. As his official biographer cautiously but correctly states,
"he was introduced to dissipations which were new to him".
They were dissipations as old as mankind and by no means
limited to princes: but news of them reached the boy's father
and in his eyes they were more fatal to princes than other mortals because they imperilled the future of royalty by possibly
weakening the "noble father of her kings to be". The Prince
Consort's letters to his intimates are full of forebodings on
this subject; he dwells much on the ruin of youth, and the fear
that his sons may "perish". By the end of the year the Prince
Consort was dead—killed, the Queen firmly believed, by
anxiety over the morals of their eldest son. Perhaps human
beings do not die from causes of that kind, but it is clear that the
Prince Consort's mind, wandering in fever, was disturbed and
confused by these escapades of the Prince of Wales. To the
last the Queen tried to resist sending for the Prince from Cambridge to see his father; it is doubtful if his father recognised
him when he arrived at the castle in the early hours of that fatal
14 December. Affectionate and tender-hearted he threw himself into his mother's arms, and exclaimed, "I will become all
you wish." But not unnaturally she could not get beyond the
fact that the closing days of the Prince's life had been clouded
by the knowledge of the Prince's behaviour. He did everything he possibly could to help her, but to her family, to the
confidential friends of the Royal Family and to the Prince Con-

sort's staff she inveighed against him, criticised his appearance and confessed to a member of the Government "it quite irritates me to see him in the room".

The death of the Prince Consort was, in all the circumstances, a dire misfortune for his twenty-year-old son. Many people at the time—and since—have argued that if the Prince had lived, he and the Prince of Wales would have come to loggerheads. Certainly he would have gravely disapproved of many of the things which were to lie ahead in his son's life, but the Prince Consort was a wise man and it is likely that he would have also tried to bring the young man forward, to see that he was occupied and to give him opportunities for showing his unquestioned talents for that side of a royal person's life which the Queen once almost contemptuously dismissed as "*fonctions et representations*". So much is of course surmise but what is certain and beyond debate is that his death at that particular moment froze the Queen in the prejudices of 1861. Until she was too old, she never lived down those feelings, so that the Prince remained outside her intimacy, excluded from her private councils and left to build a life for himself on the rather brittle foundations of London society—a world which the Queen had never liked and from which she completely divorced herself.

Immediately after his father's death the Prince wrote from Windsor to his close friend at Oxford, Dr. Acland, the eminent nineteenth-century authority on medicine: "the chaos which *now* exists and which *will* exist for a long time to come is too dreadful to think of". And then he added that "you may be quite sure we shall do everything in our power to assist and console her".[8] We may suppose that the Prince of Wales never forgot his mother's pitiful position: his recollection of that, coupled with his naturally kind heart, enabled him to endure the long years of snubbing and hard usage from his mother— treatment which was always galling and sometimes intolerable. The fact that he was outside his mother's confidence was not made easier to bear when he saw first his eldest sister, the Crown Princess of Germany, then his third sister, Princess

[8]Lee, vol. 1, p. 125.

Helena, and then his youngest sister, Princess Beatrice, usurping the place in the Queen's confidence, and inner councils which should have been his.[9] Moreover, his own rank as Prince of Wales, which inevitably gave him standing as one of the leaders of the nation, made it harder to bear the slights and admonitions from the head of the state. Some of the politicians and his own private circle of friends felt acutely this exclusion, and in justice to the Prince we should recognise the fine streak in his character which made him put down any criticism of his mother and her court, and enabled him to bear with dignity what he must often have felt acutely.

Perhaps it is the more laudable when we remember the young man's character as it was formed at the time of his father's death. Primarily his interests were social. He loved a party, a convivial evening with dancing and cards: he enjoyed good food and wine, but he was not a heavy drinker though he was a constant smoker. He hated intensive study, reading and indeed being alone. He loved chat and jokes, and enjoyed sitting up through half the night. Like all the Hanoverian Royal Family his spirits and vitality were amazing; they constantly surprised even his intimate friends. He had in him a great deal of his mother and very little of his father—though his long nose and thick lips were inherited from the Coburg family. Baron Stockmar, who knew the character of the Royal Family better perhaps than anybody else, said: "He is an exaggerated copy of his mother."[10] In that there was great truth, for his spirit and vitality unquestionably came from her.

The picture of the Prince during the forty years of his maturity when he was Prince of Wales has been drawn over and over again. He springs to our mind—portly, nonchalant, masculine, with the trim beard, the conventional clothes and the curly brimmed hats worn and flourished with just a touch

[9]Much later he found it especially irritating to see his youngest brother, Prince Leopold, who was a rabid Tory and bigoted churchman, acting as his mother's private secretary and using his position to foster all kinds of undesirable prejudices. He wrote to a friend: "Prince Leopold deliberately delights in persuading the Queen that Gladstone is the enemy of herself and the Royal Family." (Lee, vol. i, p. 514.)

[10]"The Education of a Prince", *The Cornhill Magazine*, Spring 1951.

of majesty. We recognise him with the spontaneous delight we reserve for our familiars—the Prince, the leader of all that was correct and formal in nineteenth-century England, the conspicuous personality in late Victorian life. His less reputable escapades—the occasion in 1870 when he was cited as a co-respondent by Sir Charles Mordaunt or the Tranby Croft scandal in 1891, when he played baccarat with a friend detected cheating—are likely to provide the material for reading so long as the human race enjoys skimming through easy books. Here there is no need to tell again those oft-told tales, and the reader is referred to the excellent account of those and kindred matters in the book by Virginia Cowles about the King.[11] But as we turn back the pages of those long and brilliant decades—the 1860's, the 1870's, the 1880's, the 1890's—we marvel that the Prince's mistakes were not larger; just as we are surprised that his zest for *Vanity Fair* never flagged. As we attempt to recreate it all in imagination we are reminded of a phantasmagoric game of musical chairs. Gay and smiling, as youth, man and middle-aged gentleman, the Prince runs round, waiting for the music to stop. But it never does. It tinkles on its unending refrain to the dawn of the new century. Is there in fact a harder test for character and indeed popularity than waiting for the succession? Our stern moralisers of the twentieth century may smirk and sneer but reflection suggests that for all its superficial gaiety the position of Prince of Wales for all those forty years was a little less easy than it looks—a polished floor on which a far stronger character than the Prince might have slipped. The historian can point to George IV, whose period of waiting was something similar to that of the Prince; though the analogy need not be too strongly pressed, the one completely lost his hold over the public while the other, after fluctuations, was more deeply admired in the last decade of his ordeal than in the first.

By concentrating on the skylarking and pranks, which the Prince always enjoyed, writers have perhaps paid insufficient heed to one great blessing bestowed on the Prince (which helped him enormously during this time of waiting)—his wife. The daughter of the King of Denmark, she belonged to a

[11]Virginia Cowles, *Edward VII and His Circle*, 1956.

gay and high-spirited family, bringing the Prince into an affectionate circle which within a few years was to include the
sovereigns of Greece and Russia. Queen Victoria and the Prince
Consort had always kept the old royal family, that is the relations
of George III, somewhat at arm's length.[12] The Princess, through
her mother who was descended from Princess Mary of Great
Britain, George II's youngest daughter, was thereby nearly related to the old Duchess of Cambridge. Her sister was to marry
George III's grandson, the Duke of Cumberland, who was the
male head of the Royal Family. These chance connexions were
important, for they provided the Prince with a British royal
circle independent of his younger brothers and sisters who
revolved round Windsor and the Queen. Although the Princess
had no taste for official life or for ceremonial (she was incurably
unpunctual) she did provide a domestic background for the
Prince which was happy, intense and somewhat secluded. In
1867, after the birth of her first daughter, she suffered a serious and long-drawn-out illness which permanently affected
her, leaving her lame and deaf. The Prince, who was only
twenty-six at the time, and was undoubtedly young and heedless, hardly paid her sufficient attention during this anxious
time. A country observer, a Norfolk clergyman, who saw them
together a few years later wrote: "The Princess looked terribly
pale and thin, and the Prince just as much too fat."[13] But they

[12]They consisted of the Queen's aunts, the childless daughters of George
III. The last of these ladies died in 1857. The Queen's last but one surviving
uncle, the Duke of Cambridge, died in 1850. His widow, who was George
III's daughter-in-law, lived to a prodigious age, dying in 1889. Her eldest
child, the 2nd Duke of Cambridge, who was the rather explosive
Commander-in-Chief, and her youngest child, Princess Mary, Duchess of
Teck, lived in England. She was mother of Queen Mary, and she and her
children were on the closest terms with the Prince and Princess of
Wales and their family. Yet when this Princess asked Queen Victoria if she
might have a royal carriage to take her from the station at Windsor to
Eton for the 4th of June celebrations, the Queen replied that she could have
it but "it is to be made clear that it shall not be asked for again". Princess
Mary was much beloved and she was loudly cheered in the Jubilee Procession of 1887. She said to a friend afterwards: "Yes, dear, as one of the old
Royal Family the kind public always gives me a warm welcome."
[13]Herbert Armstrong, A Norfolk Diary, 1949.

grew closer together. It was touching to see the Prince, in later life, choking down his vexation when his wife drifted in late for some important function; nor did he ever show his boredom when they visited the somewhat bourgeois Court of Denmark. A shrewd observer[14] has suggested that if the Princess had been clever like her sister-in-law, the Empress Frederick, she might have formed a rival court to the Queen as was done by the Empress and her husband during the old Emperor's life-time. But the Prince was always completely in control, and it is most unlikely that he would have allowed such a situation to develop.

The domestic background of the Prince was set against Marlborough House—the London home of the heir to the throne or the Queen Dowager for a hundred years after the death of King William IV—and his country home in Norfolk. For forty years after the Prince Consort's death Buckingham Palace was virtually unused—either as a home for the Sovereign or as a centre for entertaining. To his friends the Prince alluded to it as "the sepulchre". Inevitably Marlborough House took its place as the London centre for royal entertaining. There were the formal occasions—the garden party in the summer and the entertaining, on behalf of the Queen, of the official and diplomatic world. The Prince and Princess also did much informal entertaining where they mixed society and political personalities with leaders of science and the arts. Sunday evening was a favourite time for these parties. In 1883 Sir Charles Dilke was asked to one of these dinners, and has left a list of the guests. They were Prince Edward of Saxe-Weimar (a nephew of Queen Adelaide, resident in England), Lord Hartington, the Duchess of Manchester (they were reputed to be lovers, and subsequently married), Lord and Lady Hamilton, Lord and Lady Granville, Lady Lonsdale (a young widow), Lord Rowton (Disraeli's private secretary), H. Bismarck—son of the Chancellor of Germany who was on a mission to England—Leighton (the artist), Alfred de Rothschild and Sir Joseph Crowe, who was in the Foreign Service. The dinner was agreeable and informal, but an occasion for serious talk.

[14]Frank Hardie, *Political Influence of Queen Victoria*, 1935.

Much of the year was spent by the Prince at Sandringham—the estate in Norfolk which the Prince Consort bought for him out of the revenue accumulated from the Duchy of Cornwall while he was a minor. Here the Prince and Princess lived a family life with their children, the members of their small *entourage,* their intimate friends, and neighbours who shared their interest in shooting and fox-hunting in that "rather wild-looking, flat, bleak" countryside. The adjectives are the Queen's, and it is strange that she only visited Sandringham twice—once in 1871 when the Prince was desperately ill and then in 1889 on an informal visit. In the autumn the Prince and Princess spent some time at Abergeldie adjoining the Balmoral estate. The Prince was a regular country-house visitor—the visits often coincided with a local race meeting and were generally made without the Princess. The Queen detested his love for horse racing—a pastime which had always bored the Prince Consort. In 1870 she wrote to complain of his going to Ascot for all four racing days, and this was one of the rare occasions on which he stood up to the Queen. "I am always most anxious to meet your wishes, dear Mama, in every respect, and always regret it if we are not quite *d'accord*—but as I am past twenty-eight and have some considerable knowledge of the world and society, you will, I am sure, at least I trust, allow me to use my own discretion in matters of this kind."[15]

During these formative years of the 1860's and 1870's the Prince emerges as a family man, a man of pleasure and a leader of English society, which in its more brilliant phases has never taken very kindly to persons just because they are royal. As George IV, in youth, delighted that very critical, censorious but dazzling circle of the Whig aristocracy so the Prince charmed and led their successors in late Victorian England. No doubt much of the success of the Princes in these circles depended on their rank—but not all. We cannot picture his younger brother, the Duke of Edinburgh (not a very attractive Prince), nor the explosive Duke of Cambridge, nor even his eminently respectable brother, the Duke of Connaught, achieving that particular success. And it is only right to consider on what this was based.

[15]*Letters of Queen Victoria,* Second Series, vol. II, p. 21

Primarily of course it rested on high spirits and *joie de vivre*—but this was coupled with a kindness of heart which was exceptional. Tennyson has suggested that kind hearts are not generally associated with titles, and he was perhaps too good a courtier to go on from that and point out that kindness has never been a pre-eminent characteristic of our royal house. Yet it was the conspicuous good quality of the Prince, remarked by his friends and family alike. "He is so kind and affectionate" wrote the Queen in 1887: and on the night that he died his only surviving son, George V, entered in his diary, with characteristic terseness, "I never had a word with him in my life."

The suggestion above that kindness has never been a conspicuous quality of the English Royal House may seem severe but it has its logical explanation. Kindliness and an easy manner are not readily combined with dignity. No doubt King Ferdinand of Naples, *Il Nasone,* meant to be friendly when, in the middle of a court procession, he suddenly kicked the posterior of the courtier ahead of him so that the stately procession broke into a disorderly gallop. Friendly maybe this was but it was not dignified. The achievement of the Prince was to be kindly and friendly to all without any loss of dignity. He had a highly developed sense—inherited from his mother and father and strengthened by his European contacts—of the distinction between royal persons and the rest of mankind. For example he objected most strongly when his sister, Princess Louise, married the heir to a Scottish dukedom who was not royal. Although it was true that his own daughter was to make a not dissimilar marriage, he would probably have argued that once the precedent was started similar marriages were bound to follow. The splendour and trappings of royalty appealed to him. Though it is well known that he loved ceremonial dress (for which his figure was none too well adapted) this was only a part of his desire for dignity and decorum. The atmosphere he loved to create has been well caught by John Morley who was present at a dinner party at Marlborough House. There were forty people at the dinner and Morley adds: "there was not much noise. A band played delightful music in an adjoining room, and I should have liked nothing better than to sit without talking—enjoying the spectacle, the glittering silver and glowing gold, the superb flowers and fruit, the colour of ribands, stars, and orders, and the general presence of fame, distinction, greatness of place and power about one."[16] Another sensitive observer (Mr. Gladstone) wrote to the Queen when the Prince was lying desperately ill in 1871: "It is heart-rending to look back on that picture of youth and health, and of vigour seemingly inexhaustible, and to remember that singular combination of warmth and kindliness with unaffected and unfailing dignity."[17] Gladstone was right to emphasise the combination of these two qualities—warmth and dignity. For in combination they were unusual and remarkable. But as with all humanity the virtues of the Prince were not unalloyed. With his intimates he had a love for horse-play and a relish for misfortune in others which he should have outgrown. This was perhaps a characteristic which was Hanoverian in origin. Mrs. Sidney Webb, who despite her Labour loyalties had a keen nose for the nice distinctions of social life, once remarked that the Prince was not an English gentleman but essentially a foreigner. Mr. Christopher Sykes's admirable book *Four Studies in Loyalty* reminds us of this streak in the Prince's character, but if we blame the Prince for pouring a beaker of brandy over the patient head of Mr. Sykes's great-uncle, we likewise blame the great uncle for allowing royalty to play such tricks. And no doubt—especially as he grew older—the Prince on occasions was capable of sacrificing good nature to dignity. Courtiers of the present century are fond of repeating a story about the Prince—no doubt as a kind of cautionary tale in case royal persons should be tempted to follow the unfortunate example. He was very particular that gentlemen in waiting should not disappear at night before he went up to bed. One evening when it had grown late, he was playing cards and he noticed that one of the gentlemen was missing. The unhappy man was summoned from bed, and the Prince only laughed when the culprit was found to be the venerable Sir Dighton Probyn. Though it was an exaggeration Mrs. Sidney Webb was not absolutely wrong

[16]Morley, *Recollections*, vol. I, p. 270.
[17]*Letters*, Second Series, vol. II, p. 177.

when, after closely observing the Prince, she decided that he was "essentially a foreigner" and "not an English gentleman".[18] But such anecdotes and comments, giving a darker shadow to the picture, remind us that the elements in the Prince were, as is the case with all humanity, mixed. And in spite of faults we are justified in believing that his personal success as Prince of Wales rested on that charm of manner, which is perhaps impossible to recapture in words. Testimonies to it from his contemporaries abound. Two of these, taken at random, are impressive. The great autocrat of all the Russias, Alexander II—a formidable man not easily flattered or given to flattery—told one of the Prince's sisters how remarkably successful his visit to Russia had been, and how he had won all hearts by his courteous, kind manner.[19] And another formidable character, though of the opposite sex, was struck by the same thing. When he gave away the prizes at Miss Buss's school in North London the illustrious headmistress noted with disapproval his shortness and stoutness for a man of his age, but his manner captivated her: "he has no sort of stiffness".[20]

In addition to his manner and personality he had certain other conspicuous gifts for his position. He had a beautifully modulated speaking voice, and although jokes about his guttural accent are familiar they are superficial.[21] One of his friends always remembered an occasion when he was staying at Abergeldie, and when instead of going to the Kirk, the Prince said that he would read the service of the Church of England. His friend added, "Never did I hear the beautiful liturgy more

[18]Beatrice Webb, *Our Partnership*, 1948.

[19]Queen Victoria, *Letters*, Second Series, vol. II, p. 466.

[20]When Lord Northcliffe started *Answers*, one of the first things published was the news that the Prince of Wales was called "Tum-Tum" by his intimates because of his "graceful rotundity of person". *Memoirs of Lord Hardinge of Penshurst*.

[21]Perhaps the best of these is the picture of the Prince at a christening when he was godfather. The clergyman turned to the Prince, who was looking particularly well-groomed and well-liking, and asked whether he renounced the vain pomp and glory of the world, with all covetous desires of the same, and the carnal desires of the flesh. With emphasis, with reverence but with guttural "r" conspicuous, the Prince replied, "I r-r-renounce them all."

impressively rendered, the music of his voice, the perfect diction. . . ."[22] His gifts for speaking were natural—gifts which were striking when he came to the throne. Even as a young man he generally spoke without a prepared text. When he was twenty-three he spoke at the dinner of the Literary Fund, and Lord Russell, who was there, wrote to the Queen afterwards and told her that the Prince "had acquitted himself admirably well. His delivery was clear and unpretending without any attempt to assume the part of an orator, and all the more striking from its simplicity."[23]

That the Prince seldom opened a book is of course correct and well known. He is believed to have delighted in *East Lynne* but otherwise his taste in reading has not come down to us. Since all his friends are unanimous in telling us that he hated being left alone, he probably read very little apart from newspapers. But against this he could set a gift, which was exceptional, for foreign languages. He spoke English and German from infancy. Haldane, staying with him in Germany, noticed that he had an extraordinary command of German slang "which he used freely". On a formal occasion Haldane was much struck by the King's speech to a deputation of Germans. He asked the King when he had time to put it together. "I simply spoke what came into my head, without thinking about the words," was the King's answer.[24] His French was excellent, and he was a past master in the grace and idiomatic subtlety of that language. In addition he had a good working knowledge of both Italian and Spanish.

To-day we see the Prince most clearly as a man of pleasure—a prince with frivolous pursuits. We should recognise him at once on a racecourse—the top hat with the curly brim, the bulky form squeezed into an overcoat, ever so slightly too tight, the racing binoculars slung over the back, the kid gloves with the black, emphatic lines on the back. We should recognise him at a green baize table, producing his own set of counters, marked with the Prince of Wales's feathers—those special dice

[22]Lord Redesdale, *King Edward VII: A Memory*, 1915.
[23]*Queen Victoria Letters*, Second Series, vol. 1, p. 192.
[24]Lord Haldane, *Autobiography*, 1929.

—not loaded—but strictly personal which so shocked Victorian susceptibilities at the time of the Tranby Croft case. We see
him undergoing the cure at a German spa, puffing at a large
cigar, the short, portly legs crossed, displaying the shapely boots
which he invariably wore. But because this side of life pleased
him and because he had no sort of intellectual tastes or interests
we should only see half the man if we ignore his serious interests. Like many of the Victorian aristocracy he was concerned by the contrast between the extremes of wealth and pov-
erty. Possibly these Victorian aristocrats were more conscious of
such things than the business and middle-classes and even than
the politicians who, at that time, were largely pre-occupied with
political issues—the franchise, Ireland and our responsibilities
overseas. Certainly the Prince had opportunities of seeing things
for himself which were greater than those available to almost
any of his contemporaries. There was hardly a part of the
country which was unknown to him (except Wales, which was
unfashionable and which he disliked), and through the Duchy
of Cornwall's property in South London and through Sandringham he had direct experience of the difficulties and hardships which were endured by a majority of his fellows. He himself was a member of the famous Housing Commission which
was appointed by the Liberal Government in 1884. The
questions which he put to the various witnesses were pointed
and showed a real grasp of the problems which the Commission
was examining. The only full speech which he made in the
House of Lords was on housing, and referring to a visit he
had paid to St. Pancras and Holborn he said: "The condition
of the poor, or rather of their dwellings, was perfectly disgraceful." He added the hope that the Royal Commission would
make recommendations which were thorough and drastic.

On the important issues of the time the Prince was certainly
not unenlightened. His views could perhaps be classed as Liberal
—though they were confined within the bounds of intense
patriotic feeling, and an unfaltering belief in the destiny of the
British people. A man like Wilfrid Blunt, who resisted British
imperialism among the Arabs in the Middle East, was beyond
the comprehension of the Prince. He amusingly and inaccur-

ately dismissed him as "this disloyal and eccentric Jesuit". And yet on a visit to India in the 1870's he expressed the strongest possible disapproval of the treatment of the Indians by a type of British official. He wrote to the Queen that such things were quite wrong and much to be deplored. To a Liberal cabinet minister he wrote: "Because a man has a black face there is no reason why he should be treated as a brute."[25] Such sentiments may be commonplace in the 1950's: they were more noteworthy eighty years ago when British officialdom could still refer to Indians as "niggers".

The political character of the Prince had much in common with the opinions of Sir Charles Dilke. Both were men of the world and men of pleasure, but against that background they favoured reform and change (though Sir Charles far more violently than the Prince) and they believed in spreading the British point of view abroad (though here the Prince was far more fervent than Sir Charles). And Dilke has left us the best account of the Prince's politics that we have. He contrasted him with the Queen perceptively, pointing out that she had more brains but that the Prince was sharper. Again correctly he noticed the jingo streak in the Prince "wanting to take everything everywhere in the world". And he added this: "It is worth talking seriously to the Prince. One seems to make no impression at the time but he does listen all the same, and afterwards when he is talking to someone else, brings out everything that you have said."[26]

But the opinions of the Prince of Wales were primarily of importance because of the future, of the day when he would be king, when he would come to the throne, his opinions moulded and his prejudices sharpened by the views he had absorbed and the experience he had gained when Prince. As Prince of Wales he was in the official world but excluded from its inner councils. On the major issues of the day he was neither consulted nor informed—the Queen wished it so. His opportunities for making himself useful, for helping his mother, for serving the country were at home strictly limited. Was it perhaps

[25] Lee, King Edward VII, vol. 1, p. 399.
[26] Gwynn and Tuckwell, *Life of Sir C. Dilke*, vol. 1, pp. 500-1.

a little galling to talk to politicians on subjects where their information was official, and his speculative?

That is perhaps one reason why he sought an outlet for his political interests and capacity abroad, where the force of his mother's restraints could not be felt. As he grew older his relationships with the Royal Houses of Europe spread prodigiously. In Denmark his father-in-law was king: in Russia his brother-in-law was Czar, his sister-in-law a Grand Duchess. In Germany his brother-in-law was heir to the throne, and he was nearly related to many of the old German royal houses. The Kings of Belgium and Portugal were his cousins: he was on terms of close private friendship with the heir to the Austro-Hungarian Empire and with at least one of the leading statesmen of France.

From the 1870's on he paid a regular late summer visit to the Continent: the marriage or obsequies of a royal relation or an international Exhibition made excuses for further short jaunts. He became in fact as well informed on foreign affairs as was his father, and his first-hand experience of foreign countries gave him the authority with ministers denied by his mother. Writers would seem mistaken who attribute to the Prince elaborate schemes and tortuous policies in foreign issues. He had a single aim—that the reputation of Great Britain abroad should stand high. He hoped, by personal contacts, to smooth away misunderstandings. He had no personal ambitions but, excluded from affairs at home, he was gratified to find himself a person of consequence abroad.

Though it is easy enough to exaggerate what heads of states can do by personal contact to resolve national prejudices and rivalry, they can certainly do something to prepare the ground in which better understanding can thrive. This was especially the case in the nineteenth century whan European monarchy was at its zenith. But Great Britain, at any rate since the time of King George II, had always been on the perimeter of European Royalty.

The Russian and German royal houses were nearly related. The Austrian imperial family was closely tied to the ruling houses in Italy and Spain. Together they formed, since the days of the Holy Alliance after Napoleon's defeat, a close social circle liable to tiffs and bickering but excusing such things as inevitable among old friends. Their association could be compared with a club, to which the British Royal Family belonged but had never troubled to avail itself of the privilege of membership. The Prince took up his privilege with vigour, but it is clear that some of the regular members—especially the Germans —resented what they thought an intrusion by one whose interests were supposed to lie elsewhere.

As early as the 1860's the Prince showed that he was determined to play his part as a member of the *première partie* of the genealogy of Europe. In 1866 his sister-in-law married the Czarevitch. The Prince was anxious to go to the wedding, and he wrote to the Prime Minister: "I am a very good traveller, so that I should not at all mind the length of the journey."[27] Although nothing of great consequence came from the visit, the Prince's "ingratiating manners"—the phrase was used by the British Ambassador in Berlin—did at least heal the breach between the two royal families caused by the Crimean War. Some years later the Czarevitch, his wife and two sons spent several weeks at Marlborough House: one of the sons was in the future to be the last of the Czars and he retained through life a happy recollection of English habits and the kindness of "Uncle Bertie". In 1874 the Prince was again in Russia for the marriage of his brother to the Czar's daughter—and this was followed by a visit to England by the Emperor—the first visit of a Czar for thirty years. The Queen really approved of none of these things. She shared, with Lord Palmerston, prejudices against the Russians which were violent and ineradicable. "Oh! if the Queen were a man"—she once wrote to Disraeli—"she would like to go and give these Russians, whose word one cannot believe, such a beating! We shall never be friends again till we have it out."[28] Although the Prince would not necessarily have disagreed with these sentiments he was striving, by getting to terms of friendship with the Imperial Family, to

---

[27]It is not easy to think of any member of the British Royal Family who had visited Russia before the Prince.

[28]Monypenny and Buckle, *Life of Disraeli*, vol. II, p. 1089.

move towards a more rational relationship. The Prince was in Russia in 1881 for the funeral of the murdered Czar, and again in 1894 for the funeral of his brother-in-law. After this last visit Sir William Harcourt, who was Chancellor of the Exchequer, wrote to the Prince: "Those who are best acquainted with the difficulties and dangers which envenom the international relations of Europe must highly appreciate the great service which Your Royal Highness has been able to render to your country by the establishment, not only in fact but (what is not less important) in public opinion and sentiments of the most intimate and friendly relations with Russia. This is an experiment which has never yet been fairly tried in foreign affairs, and it is my humble opinion that there is none which is more likely to minister to the cause of peace and goodwill."[29]

Not all was on the credit side. The European activities of the Prince made him many friends and some enemies. The German dislike of the Prince, for example, was largely personal, springing from a suspicion that his private friendliness was merely assumed for political ends. His relations with the last Kaiser, Emperor William II, have been the subject of numerous books and they need not be elaborated here. Suffice it to say that there was personal antipathy between the two men—derived on the King's side from devotion to his sister who was suffering cruelly (and not in silence) from the Kaiser's behaviour. How the Kaiser viewed his uncle is well illustrated by the following extract from a letter; it was written when the Kaiser was still in his twenties and had not become Emperor, to the Czar. "We shall see the Prince of Wales here in a few days. I am not at all delighted by this unexpected apparition because—excuse me, he is your brother-in-law—owing to his false and intriguing nature he will undoubtedly attempt in one way or another to push the Bulgarian business ... or to do a little political plotting behind the scenes with the ladies." In justice to the Kaiser and in explanation of this rather odd outburst, we have to remember that the Prince was grandson to a man, known in his family circle as Joseph Surface, and closely related to the

[29]A. G. Gardiner, *Life of Sir William Harcourt*, vol. II, p. 336. British relations with Russia throughout all this period were notoriously bad.

Coburg family of whom an English Royal Duke once said:
"the spirit of intrigue exists in the whole breed". The Prince
certainly did not escape the inheritance of his blood. The talk-
ativeness, of which his parents so deeply disapproved, was
no doubt a cause of some of these feelings of suspicion when
it was elevated to the heights of international relationships.
He also perhaps seemed too deep and knowing—qualities which
invariably irritate others. But whatever the Kaiser and the
Germans may have justifiably fancied, the Prince had in reality
no deep designs: his aim was friendship and understanding,
through personal contact, with all. As early as the 1870's he
had urged Disraeli, who was then Prime Minister, to allow
his Foreign Secretary, en route to a European conference in
Constantinople, to call in at Paris, Berlin, Vienna and Rome on
his way. Officials of the Foreign Office strongly objected.
The Prime Minister overruled them writing: "I think on these
matters H.R.H. is a better counsellor than Lord Tenterden.[30]
The Prince of Wales is a thorough man of the world, and
knows all these individuals personally.... We suffer from a
feeble and formal diplomacy and there has been little real in-
terchange of thought between the English government and
foreign Powers."[31] We are therefore justified in looking on the
Prince during the forty years he was heir to the throne as a
free-lance diplomatist of much capacity and some achievement.
The great question lay ahead. When at last his mother died
would he revert to the insularity of former British sovereigns
or would the Coburger from Buckingham Palace continue to
sit down at banquets, to drive through gaily decorated streets
and to talk quietly by a glass of sulphurous water in a spa with
Romanov, Hohenzollern and Habsburg?

II

On the evening of 22 January 1901 the Prince sent a telegram to the Lord Mayor of London: "My beloved Mother,
the Queen, has just passed away surrounded by her children
[30]Permanent Under-Secretary at the Foreign Office.   [31]Lee, vol. 1, p. 423.

and grand-children." He must, in imagination, have often pictured that moment, and we may suppose that at least since the 1880's he would not have been human if he had not thought that each year might see him on the throne. When at long last his time came was it perhaps too late?

Queen Victoria's services to the monarchy and the British people are not belittled by the suggestion that her son had his own individual contribution to make, and that it was unlucky for him that the inheritance was delayed by the exceptional longevity of his mother. He came to the throne in his sixtieth year—an age when his contemporaries were beginning to think of a villa at Cheltenham, the Chines at Boscombe, or shadows across the croquet lawn at Budleigh Salterton. And it will be appreciated that his succession brought him not only the crown and the assumption of a heavy burden but the task of reviving a large part of the sovereign's duties. He was not only succeeding to the work of his mother in 1901, but to all that side of the monarchy which she had allowed to lapse since the death of his father forty years before. Especially towards the close of the Queen's reign, the authority of the Crown had been exercised by a camarilla of ladies—the Queen, Princess Beatrice, Princess Christian and to a lesser extent by those ladies of the court—Lady Churchill,[32] Lady Ely and others by whom the business of the Court was conducted. There was inevitably some antagonism between the Prince's court and the Queen's court—the virile, masculinity of Marlborough House and the harem at Osborne, as it has been uncivilly called. This was noticeable in 1892 when the Prince's eldest son died.[33] The

[32]She was born Lady Jane Conyngham – the grand-daughter of George IV's favourite – and a lifelong friend of the Queen.

[33]Albert Victor, Duke of Clarence (1864–92). He was an agreeable young man, more like the English Royal Family in appearance than his younger brother King George V. He fell in love with Princess Helene of Orleans – a Roman Catholic. King Edward, who was singularly tolerant on religious matters, seems to have favoured the marriage, and it is believed that Queen Victoria thought the young Prince might make the marriage and abdicate from the line of succession. Nothing came of this. He became engaged to Queen Mary just before his death. Queen Alexandra never really got over his untimely death, and found difficulty in accepting the marriage of his bride with her surviving son.

Queen lent Windsor Castle to the Prince for the funeral. The Queen's daughters insisted on coming from Osborne for the funeral although the Princess had asked that they should not do this. The door of their pew jammed, and the Prince sent a message that if his sister was vexed by this "she must get over it as she likes". The Prince's courtiers noticed certain uncomfortable frugalities in the castle—newspapers in the W.C.'s and not more than three lumps of suger for anyone wanting a tray of tea. "Now we know why you are all so rich," wrote one of the Prince's equerries to the Queen's private secretary.[34] Buckingham Palace and to a lesser extent Windsor Castle shared the gloom and the control by servants of any other homes during a prolonged widowhood. "As it was in 1861 so shall it ever be." But the effects of the widowhood were deeper than a mere lowering of the blinds in castle and palace. The King himself felt that the authority of the Crown had been somewhat impaired, and its splendour tarnished by the four decades since his father's death. With vigour he took up the torch from his mother, determined—so far as the monarchy was concerned—that he should reign, restore and reform.

According to the custom of the constitution he met the Privy Council on the day after the Queen's death. He made a short speech which was a model of its kind. He had consulted no one about it, made no notes, but had thought over what he should say in the train coming up from Osborne. He paid affectionate tribute to his mother and father, explained that he was dropping the name Albert from his title, appealed for the support of Parliament and the nation, and promised: "as long as there is breath in my body, to work for the good and amelioration of my people".

"I regret the mystery and awe of the old Court," sighed Lord Esher as he turned away from this first official gathering of the new reign. Dilke, always perceptive, noted that it was a meeting of men "with a load off them". The old court of the Queen, shrouded, remote, secluded, imposed a burden on the machinery of the Government and there was undoubtedly a sense of relief that there was now a man on the throne with

[34]Henry Ponsonby, *Life and Letters*, 1942.

whom affairs could be easily discussed in London. But if some thought that a measure of awe departed with Queen Victoria from the British monarchy, the King made it plain, immediately he succeeded, that there was to be a revival of the Crown's ceremonial splendour. On Valentine's Day (less than a month after his mother's death) he opened Parliament in state. He drove in George III's state coach in a magnificent procession which was received by the London crowd, still sombre in black for the Queen, with rapture. Such a spectacle had not been seen in Whitehall for forty years, and the gala atmosphere was heightened by the King's wishes that all peers, who had them, should travel to the House of Lords in state coaches. It was a last, splendid gesture of defiance from the old world of transport before it surrendered to the petrol engine. The King read the speech from the throne—a constitutional custom which Queen Victoria had declined to do since her widowhood. He showed that he was not a mere automaton, when he came to the declaration, forced on him by ancient animosities that "the adoration of the Virgin Mary or any other saint and the sacrifice of the Masse as they are now used in the Church of Rome are superstitious and idolatrous". He spoke those words in such a low voice as to be scarcely audible. He was determined that, although there was no time to alter it in his own case, his successors should no longer have to make this offensive declaration. It was never made again.

Meantime the preparations for the crowning of the King went on apace, and it was made abundantly clear that King Edward would have no "half-crownation" (as practised by his great-uncle William IV) but intended so far as it was possible to go back to the pageantry of his great uncle George IV. But the question—and it was one which exercised the private circle of the King—was how far his physique would support a very active kingship. In fact his coronation had to be postponed and the ceremonial reduced because of his alarming illness, which turned into appendicitis—in those days an often mortal disorder. The King's illness was, on that occasion, a stroke of ill-luck which might have attacked anyone. Yet in returning thanks to the nation for their prayers and sympathy the King referred to his own gratitude to Divine Providence for having "given me strength to fulfil the important duties which devolve on me as sovereign of this great Empire". His own attitude to his health is illustrated by his saying testily to the doctors when his illness declared itself in 1902: "I would rather die in the Abbey than put off the Coronation." His health always took second place to his public life. But subject to that proviso he believed in taking reasonable care of himself: for example he believed in vigorous exercise. (He would have agreed with his great grandfather George III that the Royal Family, which was full-blooded and plethoric, needed plenty of exercise.) He liked good food, but was tolerably careful of what he ate. He went to bed late (again a family trait) and like many sensible people made a good breakfast—fish, an omelette, tea and marmalade.[85] He lived well and ate well but—disappointing as it may seem to those who like to show their fellows with the less favourable side exposed—he did not "guzzle". Although in public he seemed well set-up, his health was in fact precarious from the end of 1905. Bronchial disorders advanced, and latterly he was liable to paroxysms of coughing and breathlessness.

As King he ruled his time with a routine which was unchanging. The Christmas holidays he spent at Sandringham and they were followed by a sojourn at Buckingham Palace for three or four weeks. He went to the South of France, to Biarritz, to escape the worst of the east winds. If he was back in time he spent Easter at Windsor, and Buckingham Palace was his headquarters for the summer with breaks for Ascot and Goodwood, and if need be for an official tour abroad. In August, after a week at Cowes, he went on country-house visits, grouse-shooting and racing, and three weeks in September were invariably spent at a foreign spa. He was at Balmoral for all October, and November and December were passed in London with breaks at Windsor or Sandringham for the pheasant shooting. His birthday was always spent at Sandringham. It was, as his mother in earlier days had often said, a restless life.

We know perhaps less of the private, home life of King

[85]See Lord Esher's account of a breakfast at Buckingham Palace in 1907.

Edward than of any of our recent sovereigns. Although he occasionally went alone on a country-house visit and always alone to Marienbad in September, Queen Alexandra and her unmarried daughter, Princess Victoria ("Toria") were the family background to his life. Mother and daughter, easily amused, kind, affectionate and simple had little taste for pomp or ceremony but loved the easy relationships of Edwardian social life. We see them in yachting caps, clasping pug, peke and scottie, a strange contrast to the King beautifully caparisoned in admiral's uniform: we see them on the Moors around Balmoral or on horseback in Denmark: we see the Princess taking exercise on a prodigious swing on the royal yacht, or laughing as she watches the sailors trying to play diabolo. Dear, plain Miss Charlotte Knollys, devoted Lord Knollys and the faithful Sir Dighton Probyn, his spreading white beard shown to advantage against a black, knicker-bocker suit and all the noisy Royals of Denmark and Greece that was their world. But it was not exactly the King's. We see him against their background of dogs, kodaks and pleasant little family jokes, watching it all with an easy tolerant smile—leaning against a pillar on the yacht, white-flannelled legs crossed, one hand resting affectionately on the shoulder of his favourite grandson— the future King Edward VIII, or returning to join the ladies for luncheon at Balmoral, sitting astride a broad-backed pony, enveloped in a huge cloak, looking not unlike some ancient warrior of the Glens. He was an affectionate, easy family man but on to family life he imposed his own tastes, his own interests, his own friendships. He delighted in the company of witty, entertaining women who could amuse him with the daring sallies beloved by Edwardian society. Mrs. George Keppel, Consuelo Duchess of Marlborough, Lady Londonderry, Mrs. Willie James, Lady Lonsdale and Mrs. Cornwallis West were his closest friends: they stayed regularly at Sandringham, and he met them constantly at country houses. Mrs. George Keppel was his especial favourite, and those who have read the delightful account of her in her daughter's book[36] will understand why.

[36]Sonia Cubitt, *Edwardian Daughter*, 1958.

Perhaps the following anecdote illustrates their relationship. The King, playing bridge which he enjoyed though his skill was moderate, put down as dummy a disgraceful hand on which he had pushed up his partner. Mrs. Keppel, who was thus left to play the hand looked across to him and said: "All I can say, sir, is God save the King and Mrs. Keppel."[37] No doubt those who believe that sovereigns should not attempt to combine their duties with the delights of social and fashionable life will condemn King Edward: he would no doubt reply that it was his recreation, his attempt to overcome that isolation and seclusion which can prove fatal to the best intentioned kings and queens.

On home politics the King had few of the violent prejudices of his mother; there was for example nothing in his time to match the vendetta of the Sovereign against Mr. Gladstone. His personal opinions could be summed up as not averse from changes, but entirely opposed to radical policies which might lead to bitterness and acute party conflict. Like his mother he was influenced by personal feelings. He was never at ease with intellectual men; he disliked Arthur Balfour, the Conservative Prime Minister for the first half of his reign, and his relations with Mr. Asquith were never close.[38] On the other hand the more radical Campbell-Bannerman appealed to him, and the two men got on admirably.

With the exception of Lloyd George's budget in 1909 and the approaching struggle between the two Houses of Parliament

[37]Lee, vol. II, p. 394. Although King Edward continued to use the fashionable club in St. James's (the Marlborough) which he had helped to found he did not enjoy parties from which the opposite sex was excluded. On one occasion women had to be left out from the invitations to Windsor during Ascot week, as Queen Alexandra was in deep mourning for her father. A list of these male guests was shown to the King when he came to the Castle, and he said rather ruefully: "What tiresome evenings we shall have."

[38]This is stated in the King's official biography by Sir Sidney Lee. On the other hand Asquith is more likely to be correct when he states that the frankness of the King "made our relationship in very trying and exacting times, one not always of complete agreement, but of unbroken confidence". (Asquith and Spender, *Life of Lord Oxford*, vol. II, p. 282.)

which were looming on the horizon just as the King died, he did not attempt to restrain or combat ministers.[39] He did, however, keep abreast of the whole range of Government business for—as Lord Esher once noticed—he was interested in everything. He was punctilious, and woe betide the minister who failed to keep the King informed of what he was doing. Mr. George Wyndham, when Chief Secretary in Ireland, forgot to tell the King of an appointment he was making. The Chief Secretary excused himself with the plea of pressure of business. The King commented: "The excuses of ministers are often as gauche as their omissions." He was not always amiable. He knew, as did all the world, that Lord Salisbury had been guilty of a job in appointing Alfred Austin as Poet Laureate—really in return for journalistic services to the Conservative Party. Shortly after his accession he sent Salisbury some verses of the Laureate pointedly calling his attention to "the trash which the Poet Laureate writes".

On questions which he felt were his direct concern—that is those affecting the armed services—his interventions were direct. Of all the members of the famous Liberal Government, formed at the end of 1905, he was most friendly with Haldane, who was Secretary of State for War. He introduced drastic reforms in the Army and created the Territorial Force. Of his own initiative the King summoned all Lords-Lieutenant to Buck-

[39]The approaching political storm, of which the Lloyd George budget was the warning signal, distressed and disturbed the King. Stupid people are always found who tell us that sovereigns are killed by their worries —Henry II over undutiful sons, Queen Mary over Calais, Queen Victoria over the Boer War and George V by anxiety over the future of the Monarchy. Human beings do not die so easily. That King Edward was killed by the quarrel over the Lords would be no more true than all the rest. Queen Alexandra thought that he had been killed by "that horrid Biarritz", but Conservative busybodies whispered that the Liberals had really killed the King by bringing him into the constitutional struggle between the two Houses of Parliament. Certainly this question depressed him acutely—especially the feeling that he was helpless to avert the storm which he clearly saw. Those who write him off as an idle *flâneur* would have to agree that these apprehensions were well-found. Nor did he show less foresight in sharing, with just a handful of his fellow-countrymen, the gravest anxiety over events in Europe.

ingham Palace and gave them a powerful and impressive speech, urging them to make the Territorials effective in their counties. As Haldane says, "he supported me strenuously". In fact he gave Haldane just the authority which enabled him (an advanced politician) to carry the civil servants and generals, without friction, towards a modernised army.

Over King Edward's reputation there will always remain one question mark. Was he, as the Germans sincerely believed, plotting to encircle them in Europe or was he, as some others believed, merely an outsider in Europe dabbling in their affairs from a love of mischief and a desire to show-off—backed up as he was by the Royal Navy, the Empire and Tommy Atkins? Although no doubt to the end of time we shall hear

> ... *great argument*
> *About it and about* ...

one point needs emphasis. There is no shred of evidence, either in the recorded letters of the King or any private conversation that has come down to us, that he had any specific aims in foreign policy. True he was strongly pacific and it is also true— as has been suggested in the previous chapter—that he was anxious to clear up misunderstandings and improve relations between this country and foreign powers. We can accept the fact that the intrusion of a direct British finger in the European pie inevitably gave rise to suspicion. Personal concern with what was afoot in Europe never had been a characteristic of the English monarchy or statesmanship—at any rate for a century. Moreover, the private and informal visits which the King made abroad when he was Prince of Wales became at once formal and official as soon as he was Head of the State. He was not accompanied by a Secretary of State, and this gave the impression that a new, personal and extra-Parliamentary foreign policy was being followed. It is suggestive that when in 1903, he made his first round of official visits he kept all the arrangements in his own hands, evidently fearing that the cabinet might attempt to curb him.[40] But we shall be on safe ground in arguing that the King went abroad because he loved foreign travel because he was insatiably curious, because (being human) he

[40]Sir Frederick Ponsonby, *Recollections of Three Reigns*, 1951.

loved to have a field where he was better informed than members of his Government, and because he felt that he was being of use.[41] Possibly he could be criticised for viewing all these matters of high policy from too personal a point of view. We can see how the personal aspect appealed to him from the instructions which he gave to Field-Marshal Wolseley when that distinguished soldier was sent by the King to announce his accession to certain of the courts of Europe. First he told Wolseley exactly what uniform and orders he should wear: if the Emperor of Austria did not speak in English he was to address him in French: he was warned that the King of Rumania was "a queer fellow. His wife is a poetess and they are seldom together." He was given an interesting piece of information about the King of Servia: "he has made a curious mésalliance, having married his father's mistress".[42]

Again the dislikes of the King—and they were tenaciously held—coloured his views on international friendship. He did not love his strange cousin Ferdinand of Bulgaria, who combined the Bourbon and Coburg capacity for intrigue with a wit and ability all his own. The Prince intimated that he wished to pay his last respects to Queen Victoria, but if he came to the funeral, he made it clear that he would have to be treated as a ruling prince rather than a near relative. The British Court made it plain that the funeral was not an opportune moment for raising matters of that kind. The Prince declined to come, and celebrated the solemn day by holding a great review and indulging himself with a gala luncheon. Two years later the King saw the British diplomat who had been appointed to Sofia and he said: "Tell the Prince that I do not forget the lineal ties between us, but I cannot support him till he abandons his double-faced policy." The description of the

[41]Probably he over-rated what could be achieved by personal intervention. For example he was startled and mortified when he found that his personal efforts to bring the Conservative and Liberal Parties to an understanding on the constitutional issue over the House of Lords were absolutely futile. Not dissimilarly he was disappointed to find that relations between Germany and England continued to deteriorate. He explained his chagrin on personal grounds, "I believe the German Emperor hates me."

[42]Lee, vol. II, p. 16

Prince's policy was correct, though its transmission must have taxed the skill of the diplomat. Subsequently King Edward was persuaded to ask his cousin to stay, and grew to admire his witty, malicious conversation. It was of him that he made the celebrated remark, when discussing whether he should be invited to stay: "Tell him to bring only a small suite. The smaller the Prince the bigger the suite."

His relations with a somewhat similar cousin, King Leopold II of the Belgians, remained as stormy. The morals of this sovereign caused much chatter, and it is believed that as an elderly roué of sixty-five he indulged in an escapade when visiting England for the funeral of Queen Victoria. This virtuous prince treated his daughters, whose fancies strayed beyond the straight-laced figures of royalty, with the savagery of a sultan. In addition he was viewed askance in England because of his severities in the Congo where he was an Empire-builder out of his own considerable private fortune, and an Empire-builder who did not hesitate to wield the lash. King Edward refused to go to Belgium or to have King Leopold to stay. When the matter was taken up officially by the Belgian Government the King replied that he felt himself at liberty to express his disapproval of the King's treatment of his daughters, that he entirely shared English feelings over the Congo and that, though he remembered old days, there were certain traits in the character of the King which he could not get over. He never had anything to do with him. Perhaps the critic of King Edward would be justified in saying that he treated the rulers of Europe somewhat too much as though they were members of the Marlborough Club facing a club row. Outrageous behaviour could be restrained by a rebuke and by the feeling that opinion was against its perpetrator, while friendliness and worldly wisdom could keep the club running in well-mannered amity.

After the coronation and after the King's recovery from his illness he put this to the test by the first of his official tours. In the spring of 1903 he visited Portugal and Rome, paying an informal visit to the Pope accompanied by the usual objurgations from Protestant societies at home which he ignored. In Rome he made an excellent impression. In an impromptu speech at a banquet given in his honour by the King of Italy and carried away by the warmth of his reception he said: "We have often fought side by side"—a statement which in 1903 somewhat taxed the historical ingenuity of his staff. The visit was a triumphant success, and an Italian journalist, commenting afterwards, compared the King with the sun "spreading genial light and warmth all round". The German Emperor, disturbed at the possible effect of the King's visit on the Triple Alliance (Italy, Austria and Germany), followed in his tracks. As a writer has correctly if cruelly said: "He might just as well have stayed at home."[43]

But there was a more difficult task as he moved north to England. How would King Edward be received in Paris? Knowing the city as he did and loved by Parisians as he unquestionably was, he was going there when the English were just emerging from a period when they were as unpopular as they had been in the days of Joan of Arc. We had clashed with the French in Egypt and North Africa, and their sympathies were vociferously pro-Boer in the war that had just ended. When the King arrived in the capital he drove in state with the President, his fair beard conspicuous against the scarlet of his field-marshal's uniform. Cries were distinctly heard of *Vivent les Boers* and *Vive Fashoda*—an Egyptian village on the Upper Nile which five years previously the French had tried to invest.[44] Officials in the procession blanched: the King was unperturbed. But his reception was not warm. However, the publication of a speech, which he made to the British Chamber of Commerce, when he spoke of his affection for the city "strengthened by old and happy associations that time can never efface" improved matters, and the Parisians began to thaw.

On the evening before he left, the King was entertained to a state banquet at the Elysée. What took place is best described in the words of the assistant private secretary who was with him. "At the conclusion of dinner the President proposed the King's health in a speech prepared by the Protocol. He

---

[43]F. J. C. Hearnshaw, *Edwardian England*, 1933.

[44]The long historical reach of the French mind is illustrated by the cry *Vive Jeanne d'Arc* which was distinctly heard by one of the King's staff.

was obviously nervous and had propped the speech against one
of the candlesticks in front of him, which necessitated his
leaning forward to read it. The result was that only a certain
number of people near him could hear what he said. When he
had finished, the King got up and replied in French. He never
seemed at a loss for a word and without any notes or paper in
his hand he made an admirable speech, speaking like a French-
man, which captivated all the guests. They had been accustomed
to hear a President mumbling a speech and they were carried
away with enthusiasm. The King spoke clearly and distinctly so
that all the people at the further ends of a long table were able to
hear, and this no doubt accounted for the enthusiastic ovation
he received when he sat down."[45] If it is possible to create an
alliance by public oratory then King Edward is certainly the
creator of the Entente Cordiale. But it would be more correct
to say that by a superb personal performance he caught and
illumined feelings between the two peoples which existed and
were developing.

The most controversial of the King's excursions was when
he met the Czar at Reval in 1908—a port and pleasure-resort
on the Baltic which Peter the Great had captured from the
Swedes. The King, the Queen and Princess Victoria went in
the *Victoria and Albert* with an escort of warships at the beginning of June; after a rough passage across the North Sea in
which Queen Alexandra was flung to the ground, the travel-
lers had perfect weather at Reval. While the trip could be
regarded as a family gathering—the Czar was the Queen's
nephew and the Czarina was the King's niece—critics at
home grumbled partly because it was the first time a reigning
British sovereign had visited Russia and partly because the
Russian imperial government was out of favour with the left.[46]

[45]Sir F. Ponsonby, *Recollection of Three Reigns*, 1951, p. 172-3.
[46]Mr. Keir Hardie, then leader of the Labour Party, Mr. Arthur Ponsonby
(a Liberal) and one other Member of Parliament were struck off the
list of guests to be asked to the royal Garden Party, by the King himself.
This followed their protest against his meeting the Czar. Speaking in
the democratic atmosphere of South Wales, Keir Hardie said that the
King had stood outside politics since the time of Charles I: "he had better
stay there".

Many photographs of this spirited occasion survive—the King's daughter, Princess Victoria, with her long, somewhat melancholy face, the Czarina, still beautiful and wearing a large Edwardian hat, supporting herself with a parasol, the Grand Duchesses gay in spite of their party dresses, the little Czarevitch with his sailor companion. But melancholy blurs the bright picture—for we, who survive, know that ten years later, almost to the day, all the members of this happy, dignified family were to be put to death in a gloomy villa in Siberia. We have a masterly account of the King being briefed by the British Ambassador in Russia (Sir Arthur Nicolson). The King asked a number of political questions—what were the agricultural prospects in Russia, did the Empress get on well with the ministers, what were the exact provisions of the Anglo-Russian Convention which had been lately signed, what were the Russian railways like, what were the relations between the Duma and the Government, would it be wise even to mention the Duma, what was the state of the armed forces and education, and who were the leading Russian scientists and men of letters? All this conversation was interlarded with those trivialities which fascinated the King. Would the Emperor wear the uniform of the Scots Greys or would he appear as a Russian admiral? What decorations would he wear? Would his leading courtier be content with a K.C.V.O.? The particular gift of King Edward lay in absorbing on a retentive memory the answers to those questions. Then in conversation with the Russians he was able to show not only interest but a grasp of what was being discussed. *"Ah,"* said the Russian Prime Minister, *"on voit bien que c'est un homme d'état."*[47] So far as is known the King and his nephew did not touch on foreign issues, but as Sir Harold Nicolson reminds us the greatest diplomatic victories are often won by doing nothing. The very fact that the visit —whatever was or was not discussed—was a striking success, pleasing the Russians and fortifying the Czar, annoyed those

---

[47]This is based on the unrivalled and amusing account of the Reval meeting in Sir Harold Nicolson's life of his father (Lord Carnock) which was published in 1930. The extracts do not do justice to the original to which the reader is commended.

who were absent; its very success disturbed the Germans and angered the Kaiser. "They wish to encircle and provoke us," he said in the course of a public speech a few days after the visit to Reval had ended.

Those who wish to go more closely into the political consequences of King Edward's tours will examine what the statesmen (English and foreign) have to say. Two points need to be emphasised here. So far as the King was concerned there was never any question of excluding Germany—he paid more visits to his nephew in Berlin than to any other European sovereign. Secondly, the only obvious political motive in the King's mind was to improve his country's standing with the nations of Europe—certainly not at the expense of Germany though to an extent the motive sprang from the very active and aggressive policy of Germany from the 1890's onwards. Nor will the reader overlook that visiting and expeditions were a great characteristic of the time. Entertaining was the very essence of Edwardian Europe. Even the insular English aristocracy loved to go and visit their counterparts in Austria, in Hungary for the shooting or in France for a boar-hunt. The King was enjoying what was natural for a civilised European at that time. Yachts, trains and even motor-cars opened up the Continent. He took full advantage of the mobility of the twentieth century.

For the last two years of his life the King was much depressed. The deterioration in European affairs had become threatening and was only too obvious to one as well informed as the King. In internal politics at home tempers had risen sharply and the distraction of public attention from foreign dangers to a wrangle at home over the House of Lords disturbed him. His comment, when the Prime Minister told him of Lloyd George's budget proposals, shows his feelings plainly enough: in thanking Mr. Asquith his secretary wrote: "His Majesty wishes me to ask you whether in framing the Budget, the cabinet took into consideration the possible (but the King hopes improbable) event of a European war."[48] He felt acutely that he seemed powerless either to soften animosities or to rouse the statesmen to the dangers which he vividly foresaw. This, coupled with an

[48]Lee, vol. II, p. 664.

increasing uncertainty about his health, explains why he began
to wonder if he really had the strength to continue. He spoke
to his private circle of the possibility of abdicating. We can see
something of the difficulty under which he laboured in the
accounts of his state visit to Berlin in the early spring of
1909. A German observer noted that he lost his breath on climb-
ing stairs: he fell asleep at dinner and at the state opera, and
after an official luncheon at the British Embassy he collapsed,
and the room had to be cleared and doctors summoned. But he
faced these things outwardly with *sang-froid,* so that the public
was stunned when on 6 May 1910, after an illness of two days,
he died. Queen Alexandra was in Corfu and when she hurried
home the first public intimation that the King was ill came
through the realisation that he was not at the station to meet
her. The first bulletin was issued on 5 May, and the King continued to see visitors and sign papers until the last few hours of
life.   —

Queen Alexandra arranged for a few of his closest friends in
politics and social life to see him after death. Lord Haldane,
sharing with the King the same zest for life and for its good
things, came and was strangely moved as, "I took a last farewell of my old and dear Master." John Morley—the rather
tight-lipped, puritanical radical, was also invited to the Palace.
He noted how the feeling of grief by the public was more
personal than when Queen Victoria died, and he remembered how on his last official audience with the King they had
differed over Kitchener and how, in spite of this difference,
King Edward had never ceased to be kindly, considerate, genial.
"Well, he is gone," Morley continued. "He lay as if in
natural peaceful slumber, his face transfigured by the hand of
kind Death into an image of what was best in him, or in
any other great Prince. I had known him off and on in various
relations since he was a boy at Oxford when I was; and it was
moving to see him lying there after the curtain had fallen, and
the drama at an end."[49]

When we turn from the dead king—familiar in death to
all alive at the time through the photograph which was author-

[49]Morley, *Recollections,* vol. II, p. 332.

ised by the Royal Family—to make our farewell to the living
King, we become conscious of the enormous contribution which
he made to the popularity of the monarchy. In a magnificent
and sympathetic account of him drawn by the sparkling genius
of George Wyndham we can see how he faced an official occasion and how he was gifted by nature to grace it. In the summer of 1903 he went to Ireland, when Wyndham was Chief Secretary in Dublin. When the Royal yacht arrived at Kingstown
Wyndham had breakfast with the King, and his entourage;
he narrowly escaped the mistake of seizing one of the three
covered dishes placed for the King's personal consumption.
Everyone was on edge: the ministers had from the start been
dubious of the wisdom of the visit, and the news had come in
through the night that the Pope (Leo XIII) had chosen that
moment to die. The King came in. In the interval of asking
for a boiled egg and some more bacon he said: "The Pope's
dead—of course we had expected it." After breakfast, with
only twenty minutes before he had to land, he settled down with
Wyndham to send a message of sympathy to the Vatican, to
alter some of the arrangements and change the wording of the
reply which he had to make at Kingstown. The two men smoked
cigarettes and, in Wyndham's words, the King showed "the
greatest good sense and calm, monumental confidence that all
would go right". The King was given a tremendous, jubilant
welcome the whole of the eleven miles from Kingstown to
Dublin: he was perfectly composed and as unhurried at the
end as he had been on board the yacht. On 22 July the King
received eighty-two addresses from various public bodies—
though not from Dublin Corporation which, by three votes,
had declined to present one. As may be imagined the Irish contrived to make everyone a little anxious how the ceremonial
would be observed. One man shot his address straight
into the wastepaper basket. The King was perfectly cool. "Hand
me the address," he said in his fat, cosy whisper, and then
in returning thanks contrived to give the impression that he
was surprised to find the Irish such adepts in court etiquette.
On the following day the King rode to a review. On the way
back, although he was immediately protected by his brother

the Duke of Connaught and the Master of the Horse, he was
in danger from the exceptional noise and cheering which made
the horses lining the route extremely restive. Unmoved, the King
rode on, bowing and smiling and waving his hand to the
ragamuffins who had climbed into the branches of the trees.
In spite of being in uniform he allowed himself a cigarette.
When he got back he thanked those who had ridden with him
and, as Wyndham said, "beamed enough to melt an iceberg".
He left Ireland after a visit which authority had dreaded, with
the cries echoing in his ears, "Come back. Ah! ye will come
back."[50]

Although the King, in private, was extremely genial he
was never easy-going. There is no record of anyone taking advantage of his good nature—or of embarrassing him by
taking a liberty. In fact men tended to be frightened of him.
His chaffing manner had quite an edge to it. Once Lord
Haldane, whose German sympathies were well known, appeared
at a house-party where the King was, wearing a Homburg
hat which was perhaps somewhat older than the occasion war-
ranted. To the assembled company the King explained: "See
him arrive in the hat he inherited from Goethe." He could, like
all the Hanoverian family, indulge in explosions of irritation.
But he always respected those who stood up to him. When he
was staying at Marienbad he brought a royal footman with him,
who always stood behind his chair at meals. On one occasion
the luncheon guests heard the rumbles of the storm breaking
into the thunderous question: "Hawkins! Where's the mustard?" Hawkins, who knew his master well, made no movement and simply replied: "Straight in front of Your Majesty."
The storm subsided "Oh, yes—thanks." He believed in keeping people up to the mark, and no hesitation as to whether
comment was wise or tactful would restrain him. A young
official of the Foreign Office, who was attached to him when he
was at Marienbad, kept a lady waiting for a game of golf. The
King, who was talking to her, was scandalised and said as the
offender appeared: "When I was a young man I was taught
never to keep a lady waiting." The young man, who knew

[50]*Letters of George Wyndham*, Privately Printed, 1915.

how to manage the King, answered: "Sorry, sir, but I was decyphering a telegram for Your Majesty." But if he could sometimes bark the King never failed to show gratitude. When the same Foreign Office clerk did a piece of work for him at Marienbad he was unfailingly grateful, often walking across the room before a large company assembled for luncheon or dinner to express his thanks. At the end of the Marienbad visit he sent for the young official, thanked him for all he had done, said how well the work had been done and hoped he had not given too much trouble. He then fumbled in all the wrong pockets, and gave him a minor decoration.[51]

Those who lived with King Edward and saw him every day unite in recording his most pronounced characteristic. He was intensely human. That explained why his friends were devoted to him and why his household loved him. He never posed, nor did he pretend to virtues or accomplishments which he did not possess. He never attempted to hide his weaknesses. To be king and remain a human being may seem easy enough to us looking upwards from the vantage point of humanity. Countless histories and many imaginative tales prove the contrary. The combination of the two was the enduring achievement of King Edward. We should certainly salute his memory, for with his personality, "so strong and direct" as Haldane observed, he civilised the British monarchy.

[51]H. J. Bruce, *Silken Dalliance*, 1946.

CHAPTER IV

GEORGE V

King George V was born on 3 June 1865; he died on 20 January 1936. His life was contemporary with the triumph of Great Britain, when the influence and ideals of the British race occupied the summit of the world. He reflected the essential virtues of the British people at that time, together with a belief in the self-sufficiency of all things British which also was a characteristic of his generation. "How delightful to be in dear old England again" is the recurring theme in his journal as a young naval officer.

The qualities of this great King are before the world in the fine biography of him by Mr. John Gore, which deals with his character and personality.[1] They have been further displayed against a political background in the outstanding book published by Sir Harold Nicolson in 1951. Those two books—ample, excellent and together giving a complete picture of the King—are not likely to be superseded, even in this voluble age, so that any writer on King George is conscious at every turn of his indebtedness to them. But some advantage in point of time and the absence of the severe eye which runs over all official royal biographies justifies this short, additional account of King George.

Two influences were paramount in his life. The first was Sandringham: the second the Royal Navy. The Norfolk estate, with its associations of Victorian country-house life at its best, enshrined hallowed memories for the King—memories of a devoted family-life, centred on "Mother-dear" and "sisters". "Dear Papa" was of course a part of this: but a trifle formal, a shade withdrawn he was somewhat outside their world of nicknames, banter and family jokes. King George was always

[1] John Gore, *King George V: A Personal Memoir*, 1941.

small,[2] and Queen Alexandra, who loved to tease him, in writing
a birthday letter when he was fourteen told him that one of
his sisters, on realising that he was fourteen, sighed and said
"So old: so small." The difference in the way he was treated
by his two parents is illustrated by the following anecdote. When
King George and his brother were away on a cruise, the newspapers reported that they had had their noses tattooed. The
Prince, with indignation, wrote to the boys' tutor for an explanation. His mother wrote to the boy and chaffingly
asked: "How could you have your insolent snout tattooed?
What an *object* you must look, and won't everybody stare at
the ridiculous boy with an anchor on his nose." There was
no truth in the story which arose through the boys smelling
a gigantic lily, the pollen from which stuck to their noses.[3] One
consequence of the hold of Sandringham, with its bond of deep
devotion to his mother and sisters and its close circle of private
friendship, was that this became his real world to which the
official world of royalty and kingship had been added as an
almost unwelcome intrusion.[4] Things were viewed in the same
light, we are justified in assuming, by Queen Alexandra. Indeed
Queen Victoria herself had somewhat similar feelings. After
she had been staying at Claremont, where the happiest days of
her childhood were spent, with her husband and elder children
she wrote to her uncle the King of the Belgians: "We leave dear
Claremont as usual with the greatest regret; we are so peaceable
here; Windsor is beautiful and comfortable, but it is a *palace*
and God knows how *willingly* I would *always* live with my

[2]When he died the then Archbishop of Canterbury, in a broadcast not
remarkable for reticence, referred to the conspicuous smallness of the
King's head.

[3]Quoted by Sir Harold Nicolson, *King George V*.

[4]The constancy of the King's mind to these first affections is illustrated
by the following trifling anecdote. The present writer recollects looking
at the great pile of wreaths outside St. George's Chapel after the King's
funeral. Among them was a wreath, of blazing red flowers, inscribed:
"From your broken-hearted Julie". This, which might have roused the
curiosity of the scandal-monger, was in fact from a member of the
Stonor family; she had formed part of the private circle at Sandringham
since the King's boyhood.

beloved Albert and our children in the quiet and retirement of private life, and not be the constant object of observation and newspaper articles."[5] But with Queen Victoria the monarchy was her life; domestic happiness and, in widowhood, her rather selfish life at Osborne or Balmoral were refuges which alone made it possible, in her opinion, to discharge her duties. Private life and domestic happiness loomed larger in the scheme of things for her grandson, than did the sense of being royal.

One thing fostered this—though it was scarcely noticed outside the royal circle. For forty years King Edward, as a married man, was the heir and not the sovereign: this meant that life for his family continued to be far less formal than if he had been on the throne—hedged in by courtiers and officers of state. Queen Victoria noticed this, and in a memorandum, written when her grandsons were in their early teens, she wrote: "These children have, however, the advantage of not being the Sovereign's *own* Children and therefore not born and bred in a court, which, although we always brought up ours as simply as possible, still always has one great and unavoidable disadvantage. I myself was brought up almost as a private individual, in very restricted circumstances, for which I have ever felt thankful."[6] During the formative years of King George's life he was preserved from the intrusion of too many ceremonies and too much officialdom.

The other influence which governed his character was the Royal Navy. Although the advantages of a naval training are familiar to English people, it is on the whole at its least successful in broadening the mind; on King George it had the effect of confirming his belief that things are best as they are, that the world was perfect in 1870 and 1880 and that there was no place like Sandringham in those golden decades.[7] "Dear old Sandringham—the place I love better than anywhere in the world" was how he used to allude to it. When he was twelve he and his brother Prince Eddy, joined the naval training ship —the *Britannia*—where he was for two years. From 1879–1882

---

[5]*Letters*, 16 January 1844. [6]Quoted by Sir Harold Nicolson.

[7]"How often did I hear him say, 'Well, we never did that in the olden days.' " Quoted by the Duke of Windsor in *A King's Story*, 1951.

he was in H.M.S. *Bacchante* for three years, during which he virtually travelled round the world. His promotion in the Service was not spectacular. He was midshipman in 1880, sub-lieutenant in 1884, lieutenant the following year, commander in 1891 and captain in 1893. His capacity as a naval officer was far and away above the average, and he owed little to his rank. "It never did me any good to be a Prince, I can tell you," he assured his Librarian forty years afterwards. The King indeed would have gone further, and added that as his destiny was to reign "it never did me any good to be a sailor". His eldest son has corroborated the abiding influence of the Navy on his father. The King had—he writes—"a gruff, blue-water approach to all human problems".[8]

It is a little difficult to say why King Edward VII was determined on a naval education for his sons. One motive—and it was strong—was to avoid the private tutors and elaborate personal tuition of his own boyhood. Queen Victoria had suggested that the boys might go to Wellington—the public school largely founded by the Prince Consort—but her son resisted this. Perhaps the strongest influence in the Prince's mind was the recollection that his next brother, Prince Alfred, the Duke of Edinburgh,[9] had escaped the ardours of palace schoolrooms by going to sea, and had enjoyed the life and profited from it. But Queen Victoria put her finger on the objection to a naval training for her grandsons: "Will a nautical education not engender and encourage national prejudices and make them think that their own country is superior to any other? With the greatest love for and pride of one's own Country, a Prince, and especially one who is one day to be its Ruler, should not be imbued with the prejudices and peculiarities of

[8]H.R.H. the Duke of Windsor, *A King's Story.*

[9]This strange rather taciturn Prince (he is so described by his daughter, Queen Marie of Rumania), was a big influence in King George's life. He was Commander-in-chief, Mediterranean, at the end of the 1880's when the future King was serving there. He was himself a stamp collector, and laid the foundations of the King's remarkable zeal as a collector. He was an extremely competent naval officer, but both King Edward and Queen Alexandra were somewhat apprehensive of the consequences of the friendship between his gay and unconventional daughters and their son.

his own country, as George III and William IV were."[10] King George would not have disagreed with this. Even in trifles the Navy affected his public service. When a member of his staff remonstrated with him for looking cross or bored at public functions he replied: "We sailors never smile when on duty."[10]

In his twenties the future king looked forward to a successful naval career—perhaps following the pattern of his uncle's life and achieving an important command. Had things gone normally he would probably have seen action in the First World War against the German fleet of his first cousin. We can picture him in the closing years of the 1880's with all the spring and easy accomplishment of a naval officer—boisterous, full of jokes, chaff and humour. We see him with "the dear three"—the daughters of the Duke of Edinburgh—and enshrined in the memory of the eldest as "most cherished chum of the Malta days". Then suddenly, with a decisive rattle, the Fates bring down the curtain on that happy, carefree life.

After an illness of three or four days his brother, Prince Eddy, Duke of Clarence, died from an attack of influenza, complicated by pneumonia, during the icily cold January of 1892. Personally for the future king the tragedy was appalling. "I am sure", he wrote to his grandmother, Queen Victoria, "no two brothers could have loved each other more than we did."[10] And in addition the Duke's death transformed his life, just as seventy-five years earlier the death of Princess Charlotte had transformed the lives of his great-great-uncles, the Royal Dukes. Only his own death, in the lifetime of his grandmother or father, could prevent him from succeeding to the throne. His biographer in the *Dictionary of National Biography* says that the Duke's death, calamitous at the time, "proved fortunate in the event". That opinion would certainly not have been endorsed by those living in 1892, and not the smallest aggravation of the tragedy for King George V was that his family and those knowledgeable about royal circles were doubtful of his capacity to fill the place which his brother had been destined to fill.

In 1892 Prince George was twenty-six—a practical man, gay

[10]Quoted by Sir Harold Nicolson.

and light-hearted. When, later in that year, he visited the Kaiser, that formidable man wrote to King Edward and said how sorry he was to part "with such a merry and genial guest". Later on, Lord Esher was to refer to him as the *"garçon éternel"*. But the zest and spirit of boyhood are not really a wholly suitable accompaniment for the authority of kingship. The greatest triumph of the future king was to constrain his nature to fit the monarchy. The eighteen years after his brother's death were the gruelling years when he sought to adapt himself for the position which would be his.

He was no linguist and he began by trying to master German —that language, which had taken the place of French, as a means of communication for the ruling houses of Europe. The following letter to his parents' great friend, Oliver Montagu, Colonel of the Royal Horse Guards, showed how he fared :

"My dear old Tut-Tut, ... Well, I am working away very hard with old Professor Ihne at this rotten language which I find very difficult and it certainly is beastly dull here, but 'in for a penny in for a pound' so I have no English people near me at all and speak nothing but German or rather *try* to speak.

The manoeuvres at Mayence were very interesting and I was present at them four days, their infantry are certainly splendid, but I don't think much of their cavalry as far as cleanness or smartness goes. ... Last Sunday I went to Karlsruhe to pay the Grand Duke and G. Duchess of Baden a visit,[11] which was not very amusing, as I had only seen them once before in my life, and therefore you can imagine that our conversation was not very lively, especially as most of it was carried on in German ... Good-bye, dear old Tut-Tut. Ever yr, affecte old friend George."[12] The contrast with the urbane accomplishments of his father will strike the reader.

How far his decision to marry the Princess, who was engaged to his brother, was his own is a matter for speculation. He proposed to her on 2 May 1893, and the Queen wrote to him at once: "Let me now say how thankful I am that this

[11]Beloved by his subjects the Grand Duke was known as "the friend of all the world".

[12]Quoted by Mr. John Gore.

great and so long and ardently wished for event is settled."
In her journal the Queen wrote: "I have so much wished for
this engagement", but she added that she had had a sad
telegram from the Prince's mother. The services of Queen Mary
to the monarchy are beyond the scope of this book, but their
value can to some extent be gauged by considering what
would have happened if Prince George had married another
wife—for example "Missy"—the future Queen Marie of Roumania—to whom he was at one time devotedly attached. In
the intricate political difficulties by which the King was to
be faced, a different type of woman from Queen Mary might
have been tempted to interfere, with consequences which
could have been extremely hazardous. A restless, intellectual
woman like King George II's Queen Caroline or a severe and
peppery one like King George III's wife, Queen Charlotte,
would have made the King's life impossible. He was able to
carry the burden of sovereignty for one reason only—that Queen
Mary was there to help him at every turn without any desire
to lead her own life—except so far as her intellectual and
artistic interests were concerned. She provided him with that
essential for a sensitive man of his character in his position—
an essential once defined by King Leopold in a letter to Queen
Victoria as an *"intérieur agréable".* [13]

He also prepared himself for the throne by trying to get to

---

[13]King George and Queen Mary were married in the Chapel Royal on
6 July 1893. They had five sons: King Edward VIII, born 1894; King
George VI, born 1895; H.R.H. the Duke of Gloucester, born 1900; H.R.H.
the late Duke of Kent, born 1902; H.R.H. the late Prince John, born
1905; and H.R.H. the Princess Royal, born 1897. The King was a severe
father: no doubt he had absorbed the view of Queen Victoria that no
one would tell princes the truth except their families. One who saw
both the King and Queen with their sons, when they were grown up,
said that the parents reminded him of a duck trampling among its duck-
lings. In fact they were both devoted parents but for different reasons
they were incapable of showing their feelings. When the late King George
VI was seriously ill in Buckingham Palace during the First World War
the doctor, who was sitting up with him, was surprised by a visit from
the King and Queen in the small hours of the morning, explaining that
they had been too anxious to sleep. The doctor felt like saying: "Why
can't you show the boy what you really feel for him?"

know the dominions and colonies of which he was one day to be the ruler. With Queen Mary he travelled to Australia by the Far East and back by South Africa in 1901. In the City of London, on his return from that voyage, he made the famous speech in which he urged England to "wake up" if the country wished to maintain its old pre-eminence in the colonial trade. In 1905 the Prince and Princess went to India and Burma, and in 1908 he went to Canada. Making full allowance for the "aura of good-will" which surrounds expeditions of this kind every impartial observer would agree that they were outstandingly, conspicuously successful. After his return from Australia he was created Prince of Wales in a graceful letter from his father referring to "the admirable manner in which you carried out your arduous duties in the Colonies".[14] The Prince during these years of apprenticeship was not a wildly popular favourite with the public, he was not a well-known figure in fashionable society, but he had one thing which was of enormous advantage to him—he was respected.

No King—not even King William IV—has succeeded to a more tumultuous inheritance than King George V on 6 May, 1910. Abroad the Great Powers were poised for battle: at home the political parties were fighting each other with a reckless fury unknown in English history. No human being could feel anything but sympathy for this straight-forward, courageous man hurled into a sea of troubles—a sea in which the waves and tides behaved totally differently from those on that blue water whose every movement he loved and understood. On the day his father died he wrote in his diary: "I went to B.P. at 10.15 where I regret to say I found darling Papa much worse ... at 11.45 beloved Papa passed peacefully away and I have lost my best friend and the best of fathers."[15] He had enormously respected the wisdom and political acumen of his father and, in addition to personal feelings, he was conscious

[14]The Prince's titles are somewhat confusing. He was created Duke of York by Queen Victoria in 1892: he succeeded to the Dukedom of Cornwall when his father became King and was known by that title jointly with York till he was created Prince of Wales at the end of 1901.

[15]Quoted by Sir Harold Nicolson.

on that May day in 1910 that he had lost a protector—that he stood alone, to act for himself amid difficulties and perplexities which he knew had baffled his father and which, as he was assured, had helped to shorten his life. Though King George would not have been a reader of the poems of Matthew Arnold he would have warmly agreed with that poet's tribute to his own father:

> *We who till then in thy shade*
> *Rested as under the bough*
> *Of a mighty oak, have endured*
> *Sunshine and rain as we might,*
> *Bare, unshaded, alone.*

We cannot of course tell—and it is pointless to waste time in speculating—how King Edward would have fared during the four crucial years between his death and the outbreak of war. The new King correctly saw that he could not hope to carry on the personal position of his father in Europe, and he in fact abandoned the attempt. Partly for this reason, and partly because he and his first cousin were not antipathetic, relations between the Royal Families of Germany and Great Britain greatly improved after King Edward's death. King George showed wisdom. First he asked the Kaiser to come and be present at the unveiling of the monument to Queen Victoria outside Buckingham Palace. The Kaiser was deeply moved, and he referred in accepting the invitation to the sacred hours when he had supported his dying grandmother in his arms—an experience which he said "riveted my heart firmly to your house and family, of which I am proud to feel myself a member". In his speech at the unveiling the King referred to "the strong and living ties of kinship and friendship" between himself and the Emperor. On this occasion the crowd gave the German Emperor a far more vociferous welcome than they gave to their own ruler. And then two years later he and Queen Mary went to Berlin for the marriage of the Emperor's only daughter.[16] The Czar of Russia was also present at the wed-

[16]Dynastically this wedding was of some interest. The bridegroom was the only son of the Duke of Cumberland, *de jure* King of Hanover, and the only heir in the male line of King George III. He and his family had

ding; though it was noticed that Union Jacks abounded in the streets, the only visible Russian flag was floating above the Russian Embassy. The greatest cordiality was shown to the King and Queen Mary, and the occasion emphasised the improvement in the relations between the two countries and between the two families. But in the last resort, when civilised feelings between nations collapse, the good that can be done by personal ties or the harm that can be done by family quarrels (as between King Edward and his nephew) is perhaps trifling.[17]

At home the King was possibly less successful; certainly the perplexities by which he was confronted bore heavily on him. To begin with, a very unfortunate secretarial arrangement was made. At the head of King Edward's private secretariat was Lord Knollys, a man of great capacity and perhaps unexpectedly a Liberal. As Prince of Wales King George had for secretary Sir Arthur Bigge, later Lord Stamfordham, who made an enormous (though insufficiently explored) contribution to the structure of monarchy and to the Government of the country. He had been private secretary to Queen Victoria. Understandably the King asked Knollys, who had known King Edward's mind in the current issues of home politics, to share the secretarial duties on a parity with Bigge. Such an arrangement could perhaps never have worked: it certainly did not; but the effect on King George was disastrous. Instead of receiving clear guidance he listened to discordant voices. Worried and uncertain himself, he was the victim of divided councils.

The background to the first constitutional struggle of his reign was this. The House of Lords, with rash contumely, had

---

been on the worst terms with the German Imperial Family since 1866 when they had been deprived of their kingdom after the war between Prussia and Austria. The wedding marked a reconciliation between the two Houses.

[17] The relations between King George and the Emperor were never completely ruptured. There was correspondence between the two families after the war, and when the King died the fallen Emperor sent a wreath inscribed simply "From W. II and H." (H. was Princess Hermine, his second wife.)

thrown out the budget of the Liberal Government in 1909—
disregarding the fact that it had been passed by a big majority
of the House of Commons, and that by constitutional practice
the Lords did not tamper with Money Bills. The Liberals and
their allies emphatically defeated the Conservatives at the election of January, and as the election had largely turned on the
House of Lords, that House could not expect to escape the
consequences of their crowning act of folly. But the Conservative majority in the House of Lords was vast, and unless that
House agreed to a curtailment of its power the Sovereign would
have to come into play by creating sufficient peers to swamp
the majority, or by threatening to do so. The facts very closely
resembled, in essentials, the position facing King William IV in
1832.

Before the second general election of 1910 Mr. Asquith, the
Prime Minister, asked the King for a guarantee that he would
create sufficient peers if it became necessary to force reform
through the Lords. This the King gave, acting on the advice of
Lord Knollys. Stamfordham, on the other hand, thought the
advice and action wrong, and that the King instead of occupy-
ing the independent position of a constitutional monarch was in
fact ranging himself against the Conservative opposition. A
great deal of microscopic examination has been made of everything said and written at the time, but the interest of these
minutiae largely derives from the warfare in the private secretary's office. The King always felt that he had been tricked by
Asquith, that he should never have been asked to give a hypo-
thetical guarantee and that he was a straightforward character
who could be trusted to do what was right when confronted
with the crisis. That does not seem a tenable position—at any
rate in a political impasse where the Government of the day
naturally had to know where it stood before risking its majority
in a second election in one year.

Lord Knollys seems to have felt that although a constitutional
sovereign in Great Britain has a perfect right to warn a Prime
Minister and Cabinet of dangers, he has also a duty to support
the Government of the day. This last was a motive which
weighed strongly with William IV and his private secretary at

the time of the Reform Bill crisis in 1832. Lord Stamfordham—
and he could perhaps have called in aid Stockmar and the
Prince Consort—held that the Crown was above politics and
that the King even in support of his Government should not be
asked to take partisan action. The Conservatives had felt that
under King Edward the sovereign and his private secretary had
been inimical to them. When King Edward died, Wilfrid Blunt
—that shrewd observer of what was afoot—was staying at
Clouds, the home of Mr. Percy Wyndham and his son George.
"I can see," he wrote, "that the prospect of a new and more
Conservative King is welcome in this house." Such feelings
were fairly general. And there perhaps lay the mistake of King
George. He was never a partisan: he always strove to be fair;
but a position of neutrality, when politics are boiling, calls for
an adroitness of manœuvre which was completely foreign to
his nature and in truth beyond his capacity. We may suppose
that his father, with much struggling and grumbling, would
have put the royal authority behind Mr. Asquith if it became
necessary to coerce the Lords.[18]

Several writers on the political complications of King George's
reign seem to have overlooked one point which is important.
Confronted by the alarming animosities between the Liberal
and Conservative Parties the one idea of the King and Stamfordham (who became chief Private Secretary on Knollys's retirement in 1913) was to act as mediator between the Parties. These
efforts were not successful, and it is questionable whether their
failure enhanced the prestige of the monarchy or of the King
personally. There were no very good precedents for the rather
close contacts, maintained by Stamfordham and the King, between the Palace and the Opposition. They certainly involved
the King in some dire difficulties.

Sir Harold Nicolson tells us that the papers preserved in
the Royal Archives show the King pursuing the single aim of
conciliation—"unfalteringly and assiduously he sought to

[18]One of the things resented by Stamfordham was when Knollys told
the King that he would have advised King Edward in the same sense "and
he was convinced his late Majesty would have followed his advice". Sir
Harold Nicolson, p. 138.

create good blood". The great Liberal journalist, J. A. Spender, made the same point when he described the King as "having a keen eye for the points of unity and conciliation". Yet on each occasion—in 1910, in 1913, in 1914 and in 1916—when the sovereign attempted to act as a solvent on issues where the frenzy of parties offered no solution his efforts ended in complete failure. Although King George did not directly sponsor the Inter-Party Conference in 1910, it arose from a desire to spare an untried king the full rigours of the party game. Although it seemed at one time that the idea of a coalition might spring from this conference, the idea withered and on 11th November the Prime Minister went down to Sandringham to report that the Conference had failed. In 1913, at Balmoral, the King urged Mr. Asquith to see the Leader of the Opposition (Mr. Bonar Law) with the idea of coming to an understanding over Home Rule. The Liberal Government was proposing to grant Home Rule to the whole of Ireland, coercing the North; it was argued by the Conservatives that the Government was going to force this enormous change on the statute book without submitting it to an election, and that they were only able to do this because they had mutilated the House of Lords. Asquith replied shrewdly enough that such a meeting would be either a tea-party or a bear-garden. The secret meetings of the two leaders were held but were unavailing. In July 1914 the Speaker's Conference on Ireland (for which the King and Stamfordham had been patiently working) was held in the '44 Room at Buckingham Palace.[19] At the end of three days the Speaker had to inform the King that the Conference had ended, "being unable to agree either in principle or detail". In December 1916 the King himself presided over a meeting of Party leaders at Buckingham Palace to attempt to form a government after the intrigues of Lloyd George and Bonar Law had driven Asquith from office. This was not successful.[20]

[19]This is the 1844 room called by that name after it was occupied by the Emperor Nicholas of Russia in 1844.

[20]In 1931 the King was successful in preparing the ground for the "National" Government of that year. The meeting at Buckingham Palace of Ramsay MacDonald, Baldwin and Sir Herbert Samuel on 24 August

Whether the King was constitutionally right or wrong to attempt to bridge the differences of parties by his personal intervention, and whether he was really wise to do it, is a matter for the constitutional historian, but it has to be made clear that political action is still political action even if it is crowned with the halo "conciliation".

There were, however, two personal consequences of his intervention to which the attention of the reader must be directed. The first was that the King and Stamfordham were after these experiences reluctant to take a stand against the politician. Two examples illustrate the point. A constitutional sovereign in Great Britain still has the right to dissolve Parliament or to refuse to dissolve even if his Prime Minister asks for a dissolution. In 1918 Lloyd George demanded a dissolution on the heels of the Armistice so that his Coalition Government could take full advantage of the nation's gratitude to them for bringing the war to its triumphant finish. The evils of that election, which ranks in effervescent sentiment with the khaki election in 1900, are too familiar to need stressing. The Sovereign would have been perfectly justified in postponing the election for some months, so as to give normal political feelings a chance to assert themselves, and the disturbance of the war years to settle. Certainly the King attempted to warn Mr. Lloyd George of the objections to an election at that time. Sir Harold Nicolson quotes in full Lord Stamfordham's memorandum describing the interview between the King and his Prime Minister. In passing the reader may note that the King referred to the Khaki Election, which brought back the Unionists "on a fictitious vote" but "ended in ruining them". The warning was prescient. Lloyd George persisted in the election: won a resounding triumph "on a fictitious vote", left office four years later never to return. This was certainly an occasion when the difficulties of the time and the verdict of history would have

1931 was decisive. Whether MacDonald would, without royal pressure, have taken part in such a government is open to question. Whether the events of that St. Bartholomew's Day were so benign in their influence on party politics during the 1930's as some writers have supposed is likewise open to question.

justified the King in refusing the Prime Minister's request. Not dissimilarly in 1924 the King would have been wise to refuse Mr. Ramsay MacDonald's request for a dissolution after less than a year in office. There had been two General Elections in the two years since 1922, and it would have been understood by the public if the King had declined to dissolve. Probably he was largely influenced by the apprehension that he might be accused of being unjust to MacDonald and the Labour Party. He marshalled his arguments against a dissolution but Mac-Donald was headstrong and brushed them to one side. The King's action in agreeing to a dissolution has been much criticised, and his action then has probably made it difficult for his successors to use this sanction.

The other personal consequence of the political experiences in the early part of his reign was that, although he was desperately anxious to remain outside the party battle-ground it could be argued that he did not in fact remain outside, and, as has already been suggested, the very fact that his attempts to conciliate were unsuccessful did somewhat diminish the authority of the Crown and, what is more to the point, his own personal authority. It is inconceivable that any political leader could have spoken to King Edward VII as Bonar Law spoke to King George after a dinner-party at Buckingham Palace on 3rd May, 1912. The Conservative Leader told him that he would either "have to accept the Home Rule Bill, or dismiss your ministers and choose others who will support you in vetoing it: and in either case half your subjects will think you have acted against them". The King went red. Ruthlessly the Conservative went on: "Have you ever considered that, Sir?" Triumphantly Bonar Law wrote to a colleague: "I have given the King the worst five minutes he has had for a long time."[21] It has to be confessed that like his great-great-uncle, King William IV, he gave an impression of vacillation which laid him open to some criticism and attack.

He minded acutely. For all his bluffness and joviality his nature was tenderly sensitive. Lord Esher, who was at Windsor

[21]Quoted by Sir Harold Nicolson.

when the Home Rule crisis was at its height, recorded: "the King is in low spirits and lies awake at night". And even more to the point when Esher ventured to remonstrate with him, urging him not to worry himself to death, the King was moved and "turned abruptly away with some emotion".[22]

One of his naval comrades, Admiral Lord Wester Wemyss, wrote to him: "I often look back at the happy days of long ago, and there forms itself before my mind a picture of gun-rooms, of old mess-mates, and of youths without care or anxieties. Then my mind turns to the present and I see Your Majesty transformed from the cheery midshipman into the Sovereign, with all the load of anxiety, trouble and responsibility, and I cannot help feeling much moved."[23] The King would surely have endorsed the amusing remark of the last King of France that it was really better to work for a living than be King of England.

How was it that a reign which did not begin auspiciously for the monarchy ended in a golden haze? How was it that the respect which the public felt for King George turned to affection when the reign closed? He himself made reference to the public feelings for him when on the day of his Silver Jubilee he said this in his broadcast: "I can only say to you, my very dear people, that the Queen and I thank you from the depths of our hearts for all the loyalty—and may I say so?—the love, with which this day and always you have surrounded us." In spite of all the difficulties of his reign—the political ferocity of 1910–14, the four years of war, the decade of industrial unrest which

[22]King George's health was not robust. For all his love of naval life he was afflicted by sea-sickness and his constitution was perhaps permanently affected by the typhoid fever which attacked him in 1891. Lord Esher noted, when he was still Prince of Wales that he did not look well. "His dyspepsia gives him so much trouble. He is now on a rigid diet, and it does not suit him. He is not strong." He suffered from colds and bronchitis. In November 1928 he became desperately ill with acute septicaemia, and he was not sufficiently restored to return thanks for his recovery until the following summer. Thereafter he was obliged to take great care of his health.

[23]Quoted by Sir Harold Nicolson.

followed it and the financial *débâcle* and unemployment of the 1930's accompanied by dark clouds abroad—the monarchy flourished and grew stronger. Strangely enough they helped it. From the chaos of the world around them the nation turned with increasing devotion to the one stable institution in their midst. As they watched the great Houses of Europe—the empires of Austria-Hungary, Germany, Russia and Turkey— with all their lesser potentates—Grand Dukes, electors, margraves, serene highnesses, caliphs, moguls and chams—being swept up like the leaves of autumn in 1918—they were proud of the abiding majesty of the British throne. And with such feelings, as Sir Harold Nicolson has reminded us, was a sense of reverence that we had "this emblem of continuity", "this symbol of patriotism" in a rapidly dissolving world. Yet these were merely the adventitious advantages of the time.[24]

Although the subject deserves more detailed treatment than is possible in a book of this kind, there was—in spite of the brilliant façade of King George's reign—a weakness in the position of the monarchy which developed apace. Reference has already been made to the sharp decline in the political powers of the Crown. Political influence (though it was very adroitly used by the King's private secretary—Lord Stamfordham) masked the decline but was no substitute for the reality. At the same time the mutilation of monarchy in Europe and the natural (though exaggerated) revulsion of opinion against continental royalty after the 1914 war meant that the English Royal Family was dangerously isolated. The old conception of royalty as a closed corporation—that circle in which the King's father had moved

[24]Mr. Gore has pointed out that King George was seen and heard by his peoples to a far greater extent than were his predecessors. Queen Victoria, after 1861, only went to a very few functions outside London or Windsor. King Edward might go to an industrial town if it fitted in with one of his country-house visits. King George and Queen Mary began the systematic visiting of the great centres of population during the First World War, and this was continued, so far as the King's health allowed, to the end of the reign. The work of King George and Queen Mary, in an increasingly democratic nation, undoubtedly spread the personal popularity of the monarchy, and this was helped by the similar functions undertaken by the Prince of Wales.

so easily and resplendently—was shattered.[25] As a result of a
very silly outcry—largely engineered from Fleet Street—the
King abandoned his German titles and name in 1917. The
House of Saxe-Coburg-Gotha became Windsor. A Bavarian
nobleman of the old regime has observed wittily enough: "The
true royal tradition died on that day in 1917 when, for a mere
war, King George V changed his name."

The King and his advisers began to wonder whether these
violent and sudden changes in the position of monarchy might
not induce people—at a time when all institutions were being
called in question and when the axe of economy was being
freely wielded over all the branches of government—to question
whether the ancient British throne was in keeping with the
spirits of the times. Many shrewd and true friends of the monarchy were only too conscious of the danger.[26] The King and
his immediate advisers seem to have decided that to meet the
challenge of the new world the King and the Royal Family
must increasingly display themselves throughout the country
and the Empire. A boyish and delightful letter from the Prince
of Wales to his father, which was written at the end of the war,
shows what was in the wind.

5 November 1918

Dearest Papa,
. . . There seems to be a regular epidemic of revolutions
and abdications throughout the enemy countries which
certainly makes it a hard and critical time for the remaining
monarchies; but of those that remain I have no hesitation
in saying that ours is by far the most solid tho of course it
must be kept so and I more than realise that this can only
be done by keeping in the closest possible touch with the
people and I can promise you this point is always at the

---

[25]In September 1914 the Czar told the French Ambassador that he
thought the war "a terrible blow to the monarchical principle". He was
not wrong.

[26]See the *Life of George VI*, by J. M. Wheeler Bennett, p. 159, and
also the perceptive article in *The Times Literary Supplement*, 17 Oct.
1958.

back of my mind and that I am and always shall make
every effort to carry it out as I know how vitally it will influence the future of the Empire ! ! I'm sure you won't mind
when I tell you that I'm out the whole of every day seeing
and visiting *the troops* i.e. *the people* ! ! ! !

I remain dearest Papa your most devoted son

DAVID[27]

But did a deliberate policy of this kind, once started, set
the monarchical machine on a course from which there was no
return? What would happen if in the course of nature a
sovereign came to the throne who was studious, hated crowds
or was not robust? Did not this recurring parade of individuals
fling open the door to curiosity about the inner and private life
of royal persons which could become intolerable? Was it possible for any future sovereign to recapture the more serious side
of the monarchical tradition? Those are questions which remain unanswered, problems which abide. We should remember
that they are rooted in the reign of King George V.

The personality of King George is, of course, the true explanation of his hold over the public imagination. Some people
might be tempted to argue that a sovereign has only to wait, and
at the end of his or her life the public turn to them with ever
increasing affection and awe—with the feelings which we may
suppose fill the mind of a forester as he glances at some venerable trees in his care, which had endured the storms and hazards
of the years. Queen Victoria certainly illustrates the argument.
But there are examples on the other side. The old Henry VIII
lost all the popularity of the brilliant youth. Louis XIV, after his
phenomenal reign of seventy-two years, was regarded as the
cause of the sufferings and misery of his country and himself
sadly referred to the brilliant days of his reign—"when I was
really King". Some of the feelings of the public for George III,
at the end of his long reign, were epitomised in the familiar and
savage lines of Shelley and Byron.

Though a long reign may not be the secret of a sovereign's
popularity, the twenty-five years of King George gave time for

[27] *A King's Story: Memoirs of the Duke of Windsor, 1951.*

the public to grow fond of him, to see for themselves those fine qualities of courage and good sense which distinguished him. Although twenty-five years may seem a short span compared with the reign of King George III or of Queen Victoria, the King by clinging always to the habits of his youth seemed in the 1930's a survivor from a more distant, more ordered civilisation. His fashion in clothes was extraordinary. He always wore his trousers pressed at the side (as had his father before him) and his gloves, with deep cut seams on the back which were fashionable in Paris of the Second Empire, must have taxed all the resourcefulness of the royal haberdasher. Any man coming to see him—even his sons—invariably had to wear a frock coat. Looking out of the window he saw a member of his court coming to Buckingham Palace in a bowler hat, instead of the regulation silk one, and he exclaimed: "What do you mean by coming here in that rat-catcher fashion?"[28] On another occasion he said to a friend that he simply could not understand why people made so much fuss over London traffic. "If I want to cross the road in Piccadilly I just put up my stick and walk over." He could not believe that things had changed since he crossed the road in that fashion thirty years earlier, in the happy days of horse buses and hansom cabs. But in the stern life of the 1920's and 1930's these foibles were endearing.

His grandfather, the Prince Consort, said on one occasion that English people loved to have an authority whom they could quote—a character about whom they could spread anecdotes; such anecdotes need not necessarily be authentic—provided they fitted the personality of the person in question. The Prince had in mind the Duke of Wellington.[29] King George was, in his generation, such an authority. The upper and professional classes enjoyed spreading examples of his bluff wit and his outspoken way of cutting through humbug and hypocrisy. Indeed the official classes at the time turned to him with almost idolatrous affection—a feeling which, in the long run, was not in the best interests of the monarchy. Whitehall adopted an

---

[28]Quoted by Mr. Gore.

[29]No doubt the many contemporary anecdotes about Sir Winston Churchill are in keeping with such a theory.

almost protective attitude towards him. "His Majesty must not be depressed by foreign symptoms" decreed the leaders of the National Government.[30] The Church regarded him as her own, and Printing House Square in his time began to weave its web of the "mystique" of monarchy. They were freezing the institution to fit the occupant of the moment. So successfuly did they do this that at a meeting of the cabinet at the time of the discussions about Mrs. Simpson the Home Secretary was heard to moan: "What we want is another Queen like Queen Mary." These simple-minded worthies wanted and created the ideal of a sovereign divorced from personality. For these reasons King George left his successor a difficult task—indeed it was an impossible one for a sovereign not prepared to walk between the lines patiently marked by Whitehall, Printing House Square, Lambeth Palace and the apartments of St. James's Palace. Those who occupied these seats of power and influence had almost imperceptibly thrown their shadow across the throne till they could cry to its occupant "Conform or Perish".

This was certainly neither the wish nor the intention of King George—but it was a consequence of his character and particular contribution to the monarchy. "I am a very ordinary man" he is believed to have said to a friend at the time of the Silver Jubilee. That was true. And it was perhaps the sight of an ordinary man battling with extraordinary difficulties which changed the respect of 1910 into the devotion of 1935. For the closer knowledge of the man which came with his reign of twenty-five years showed the public a character whom they could understand. He said exactly what was in mind, with a certain impatience of remonstrance or interruption, but perhaps without believing that he would be taken entirely seriously. When he heard that the wife of one of his former Prime Ministers was writing her autobiography he gave authors a comprehensive condemnation with the assertion that "people who write books ought to be shut up". One one occasion he was sent by the Foreign Office a long memorandum, which had been compiled by Lord Vansittart. When he next saw that devoted man he called out: "A very interesting memorandum. I have read

[30]Quoted by Lord Vansittart in the *Mist Procession*.

It—not all of it, of course." Sir Anthony Eden went to see him at Buckingham Palace to discuss some outstanding issues of foreign policy. The band was ready to play in the Palace court-yard, and the King told his visitor that he had given orders that they were not to start playing till he sent word. He then held forth for some time, expressing with characteristic vigour, his views of foreign countries and their governments. His harangue ended, he rang the bell and asked the band to start. The Foreign Secretary—his turn for the conversation having come—was left to contend, as best he could, with drum, bassoon, trumpet and trombone.

The King enjoyed a jest. He liked to hear and retail stories which, since the infancy of the Royal Navy, have beguiled officers and men through the ardours of a long spell at sea. One member of the cabinet in the 1930's, Mr. J. H. Thomas, used to delight the King with these rather risqué tales. After his serious illness in 1928, Mr. Thomas told him one of his stories and the King laughed so uproariously that he interrupted the healing of the wound where the doctors had operated. But it would be quite wrong to leave the impression that the King's humour was mere ribaldry. He loved chaff and banter but he had the essential ingredient for any real sense of humour—he enjoyed telling a story against himself. Every day, at half-past nine in the morning, he spoke on the telephone with his sister, Princess Victoria.[31] They liked to jest with one another to the delight of the telephone operator at Buckingham Palace. "Good morning, you old fool," began the Princess. The King loved to tell how the operator broke in and said: "Excuse me, your Royal High-ness, but I have not connected you with His Majesty yet."[32] He also enjoyed an episode which happened when he was stalking in Scotland. A fairly easy shot came his way. He missed. Turn-ing to the stalker he said "Take this damned rifle away. Never let me see it again." "Yer Majesty," the stalker replied, "den-na waste yer breath damning the rifle. It was a verra bad shot." His humour was occasionally mischievous and did not always spare those he most deeply loved. On one occasion he was

[31]Queen Mary would never in any circumstances use the telephone.
[32]Told by Mr. Gore.

asked how he was, and he answered, "I am better—but I am not strong enough to walk round the British Industries Fair with the Queen."[33]

These, and countless other anecdotes of the same kind, spread throughout British society the impression of the King as he really was—a human being with an understanding of his fellows and an abiding sympathy for them. Without deliberately intending it he was able to project his personality on to the mind of his subjects. Could anything be more effective and—because the reader knew it to be true—more warming than his message to the soldiers on the Western Front during the First World War? "I cannot share your hardships, but my heart is with you every hour of the day." We may be sure that it was.

[33]Told by Mr. Gore. Queen Mary's marathon performances at this Fair were greatly admired, and freely commented on by the Press.

A SELECT BIBLIOGRAPHY

The weight of books on the years from 1830 to 1936 is prodigious : if the reader is not to be bowed to the ground by this, he should turn first to three foundations essential to his security. They are *The Age of Reform* (1815–70), by E. L. Woodward 1938 : *England 1870—1914*, by R. C. Ensor, 1936; and *Early Victorian England*, 2 vols, edited by G. M. Young, 1934, and containing, as a last chapter, a masterly survey of the age by the editor. The first two carry exhaustive bibliographies which really give general readers all that they require. The last has a generous sprinkling of authorities in footnotes; many of these were added by the editor, G. M. Young, and bear the mark of his comprehensive reading. Since this book was written the addition of an ultimate volume—*England 1914—45* by Mr. A. J. P. Taylor—to the Oxford histories strengthens conspicuously and authoritatively the foundations to which I refer above.

What follows are merely the chances of personal preference or of personal reading. Over the whole period the *Dictionary of National Biography* and the *Annual Register* are straightforward to use and packed with fascinating information.

The many biographies of the Sovereigns of this period are sufficiently clear from the text. But the reader will bear in mind that since this book was written there have been important additions to the recent history of the royal family which are essential reading. They are *Queen Mary* by James Pope-Hennessy, *King Edward VII* by Sir Philip Magnus, *Queen Victoria* by Lady Longford, *Royal George* by Giles St. Aubyn, *King William IV* by Philip Ziegler, and *Dearest Child* edited by Roger Fulford. In all these books there is much material previously unpublished. Also valuable is Christopher Hibbert's broad canvas of court life—*The Court at Windsor*. The correspondence of Earl Grey with William IV, edited by the third Lord Grey and published in 1867, should perhaps be mentioned, since it shows the serious side of the King and puts

him in a favourable light. It should be read in conjunction
with J. R. M. Butler's *Passing of the Great Reform Bill*, 1914,
and the admirable life of Lord Grey of the Reform Bill written
by Professor G. M. Trevelyan.

The politics of the period have inspired a number of fas-
cinating biographies. The outstanding ones are John Morley,
Life of Gladstone; Monypenny and Buckle, *Life of Disraeli*;
G. M. Trevelyan, *Life of John Bright*; J. A. Spender, *Campbell
Bannerman*; A. L. Kennedy, *Lord Salisbury*; A. G. Gardiner,
Sir William Harcourt; Mrs. Edgar Dugdale, *Life of Arthur
Balfour*; Spender and Asquith, *Lord Oxford and Asquith*;
Robert Blake, *The Unknown Prime Minister*; Lord Grey of
Fallodon, *Twenty-five Years*; Lord Haldane, *Autobiography*;
and the two graceful books about Lord Melbourne written by
Lord David Cecil, *The Young Melbourne* and *Lord M. Lord
Randolph Churchill*, by his son Sir Winston, is an important
book for the understanding of nineteenth-century Toryism. Mr.
Philip Guedalla's life of the Duke of Wellington will be found
helpful, as will Lord Anglesey's excellent portrait of the first
Marquess of Anglesey—*One Leg.*

General books essential for an understanding of the inner
working of public life are *The Greville Memoirs*, 1938 edition
by Lytton Strachey and R. Fulford; Walter Bagehot, *The
English Constitution* and *Biographical Studies*; G. D. H. Cole,
Short History of the Labour Movement; Sydney and Beatrice
Webb, *History of Trade Unionism*; Beatrice Webb's Diaries
and Autobiography (4 vols.), *My Apprenticeship*; *Our Partnership*; *Diaries, 1912—24*; *Diaries, 1924—32*. An excellent book
in the same field is R. W. Lyman's *First Labour Government*;
Lord Beaverbrook's two books, *Politicians And The War* and
Men and Power, are important. Three books on the political
emancipation of women are Millicent Fawcett, *History of
Suffrage Movement*; Sylvia Pankhurst, *The Suffragette Movement*, 1931; and *Votes for Women*, by Roger Fulford.

Three important books on economics are J. H. Clapham,
Economic History of Modern Britain, 3 vols.; C. R. Fay, *Great
Britain from Adam Smith to the Present Day*, 1928; C. Booth,
Life and Labour of the People of London, 8 vols.

The bibliographies of E. L. Woodward's and R. C. K. Ensor's admirable histories will give readers all they need on literature and the arts. The importance of religion in this period is emphasised and the reader is recommended to J. H. Overton, *English Church in the 19th Century*; J. H. Newman, *Apologia Pro Vita Sua*; J. W. Burgon, *Lives of Twelve Good Men*; Walter Houghton, *The Victorian Frame of Mind*.

Finally a group of books which the present writer has found especially helpful: *Story of My Life*, Augustus Hare (6 vols.); *My Recollections*, by the Countess of Cardigan; *Autobiography*, Margot Asquith; *Life of Edward Marsh*, by Christopher Hassell; *Life of Hugh Walpole*, by Rupert Hart-Davis; Lady Diana Cooper's Memoirs in the course of publication; and, conspicuously useful, Sir Osbert Sitwell's splendid volumes of reminiscences, *Left Hand, Right Hand!*, *The Scarlet Tree*, *Great Morning*, *Laughter In The Next Room* and *Noble Essences*, and the equally delightful autobiography of Sir Lawrence Jones—*A Victorian Boyhood*, *Edwardian Youth* and *Georgian Afternoon*.

INDEX

Fontana Paperbacks: Non-fiction

Fontana is a leading paperback publisher of non-fiction. Below are some recent titles.

- ☐ THE LIVING PLANET David Attenborough £8.95
- ☐ SCOTLAND'S STORY Tom Steel £4.95
- ☐ HOW TO SHOOT AN AMATEUR NATURALIST Gerald Durrell £2.25
- ☐ THE ENGLISHWOMAN'S HOUSE
    Alvilde Lees-Milne and Derry Moore £7.95
- ☐ BRINGING UP CHILDREN ON YOUR OWN Liz McNeill Taylor £2.50
- ☐ WITNESS TO WAR Charles Clements £2.95
- ☐ IT AIN'T NECESSARILY SO Larry Adler £2.95
- ☐ BACK TO BASICS Mike Nathenson £2.95
- ☐ POPPY PARADE Arthur Marshall (ed.) £2.50
- ☐ LEITH'S COOKBOOK
    Prudence Leith and Caroline Waldegrave £5.95
- ☐ HELP YOUR CHILD WITH MATHS Alan T. Graham £2.95
- ☐ TEACH YOUR CHILD TO READ Peter Young and Colin Tyre £2.95
- ☐ BEDSIDE SEX Richard Huggett £2.95
- ☐ GLEN BAXTER, HIS LIFE Glen Baxter £4.95
- ☐ LIFE'S RICH PAGEANT Arthur Marshall £2.50
- ☐ H FOR 'ENRY Henry Cooper £3.50
- ☐ THE SUPERWOMAN SYNDROME Marjorie Hansen Shaevitz £2.50
- ☐ THE HOUSE OF MITFORD Jonathan and Catherine Guinness £5.95
- ☐ ARLOTT ON CRICKET David Rayvern Allen (ed.) £3.50
- ☐ THE QUALITY OF MERCY William Shawcross £3.95
- ☐ AGATHA CHRISTIE Janet Morgan £3.50

You can buy Fontana paperbacks at your local bookshop or newsagent. Or you can order them from Fontana Paperbacks, Cash Sales Department, Box 29, Douglas, Isle of Man. Please send a cheque, postal or money order (not currency) worth the purchase price plus 15p per book for postage (maximum postage required is £3).

NAME (Block letters) _____

ADDRESS _____

_____

_____